TALES
OF
TERROR

MEDIA AND SOCIETY SERIES
J. Fred MacDonald, General Editor

TALES
OF
TERROR

Television News
and the Construction
of the Terrorist Threat

Bethami A. Dobkin

PRAEGER

New York
Westport, Connecticut
London

Library of Congress Cataloging-in-Publication Data

Dobkin, Bethami A.
   Tales of terror : television news and the construction of the
terrorist threat / Bethami A. Dobkin.
     p.   cm.—(Media and society series)
   Includes bibliographical references and index.
   ISBN 0–275–93981–2 (alk. paper)
   1. Television broadcasting of news—Political aspects—United
States. 2. Terrorism in the news—Political aspects—United States.
3. Press and politics—United States—20th century. 4. Journalism—
United States—Objectivity—20th century. I. Title. II. Series.
PN4784.T4D6   1992
302.23′45—dc20   91–28772

British Library Cataloguing in Publication Data is available.

Library of Congress Catalog Card Number: 91–28772
ISBN: 0–275–93981–2

First published in 1992

Praeger Publishers, 88 Post Road West, Westport, CT. 06881
An imprint of Greenwood Publishing Group, Inc.

Printed in the United States of America

The paper used in this book complies with the
Permanent Paper Standard issued by the National
Information Standards Organization (Z39.48–1984).

10 9 8 7 6 5 4 3 2

For my parents

Contents

Preface

As I watched the television accounts of the recent Persian Gulf War, I was mesmerized by the news stories and video images that danced on my screen. I read daily newspapers and weekly magazines, I listened to extensive radio coverage and academic debates, and I tried to consume every source of mediated information within my reach. As an educator, I introduced discussions about the conflict in my classes and spoke at public lectures and conferences about the relationship between television news and foreign policy. But few of these activities helped to quell the unease that had grown as I watched the networks struggle to provide live, dramatic coverage that would please most of their viewers, most of the time.

We did not fight any officially declared wars in the 1980s, but we did fight a war against terrorism. Terrorists became this country's archenemies, and the "scourge of terrorism" is still used as an instant justification for foreign policy gestures, funding for special programs, covert operations, and military intervention. As a public, we support these actions in the face of an enemy we do not understand and rarely see—except on television.

Television serves as the primary source of information about foreign affairs for most Americans, a situation that has prompted much research and concern. This book is my attempt to assess those concerns in the context of television news coverage of terrorism. Some of the findings may sound familiar, but others may cause readers to see the performance of television news (and incumbent administrations), particularly during times of foreign conflict, in a different light.

This book is not meant as an indictment of television, or even as a lengthy criticism of the American Broadcasting Corporation, the network that served as the focus for this study. It points instead to limitations of television journalism as currently practiced and the implications of that practice for our assessment of U.S.

foreign policy. Additionally, it is not an apology for terrorists or an implicit plea for leniency when dealing with them. Rather, this study examines the limits of the ways we come to understand the terrorist threat and our responses to it. And it is only a beginning.

Every beginning involves the synthesis of many voices. The ample bibliography provided here gives an indication of the thought that informed this book. But at a more substantial level, that of daily experience, several people lent their support and encouragement and deserve to be mentioned here. I have dedicated this book to my parents for their unwavering enthusiasm and affection. David Sullivan deserves more gratitude than I can express here for his patience, understanding, and critical insight. Jane Blankenship has continued to offer words of wisdom about this project and others.

Any detailed analysis of violent, terrifying, images and actions strains not just the researcher but also those around her. Thanks are due to Eileen McNutt, Amy Loomis, Daniel Sheehan, Fred MacDonald, the Department of Communication Studies at the University of San Diego (Cathy Joseph, Carole Logan, Roger Pace, Linda Perry, Larry Williamson), and my students. Perhaps the most inspiration has come from my family, for they have cultivated my belief that the kind of work undertaken here is not only worthwhile, it is an integral part of the struggle to make the world a better place.

This book is only a small step in that direction. In that spirit, I hope that the insights offered here help to alleviate the suffering of all victims of political violence, at home and abroad.

1

Introduction: Television, Terrorism, and Public Reality

On April 15, 1986, 33 U.S. Air Force and Navy fighter-bombers launched a retaliatory air raid on Libya, dropping 227-kilogram and one-ton bombs on targets in Tripoli and Benghazi. Years of frustration with highly publicized and sensational terrorist acts had led the United States to send a military message to a perceived sponsor of terrorism, Libyan leader Muammar Qaddafi. The number of casualties resulting from the strike was not immediately reported, but shortly after the bombing Libyan Staff Major Abdul Salaam Jalloud reported that 37 people had been killed. Thirty-six of those people were civilians. An additional 93 people were injured.

American support for the action was overwhelming. Americans wanted swift and strong military retaliation after having been plagued for a decade with horrifying acts of terrorism aimed at U.S. citizens. Opinion polls reflected this public sentiment; when the United States bombed Libya, 71 percent of the American public supported the air raid. Paradoxically, though, less than a third of those polled believed the bombing would result in fewer incidents of international terrorism. In fact, over half of those polled thought the retaliatory bombing would either have no effect (23 percent) or would increase the amount of terrorism (39 percent) (Falk, 1986). These responses expressed the humiliation created by terrorism and the anger of citizens in a "nation held hostage." The American public did not want a solution to international terrorism; they wanted retribution.

Public support for military responses to terrorism has continued. In October 1990, prior to the first U.S. air raids against Iraq, Americans ranked terrorist actions among the strongest reasons for support of immediate military action in the Persian Gulf. Of those polled, 67 percent favored military involvement "if terrorists loyal to Iraq kill Americans anywhere," whereas only 43 percent supported such action "if Iraq refuses to withdraw from Kuwait" (Yang, 1990).

Public frustration with terrorism has grown since November 1979, when Iranians took 66 hostages at the U.S. embassy in Tehran. On January 20, 1981, as the hostages were released, President Ronald Reagan was simultaneously sworn into office. From the time of Reagan's 1981 inaugural address, when he unveiled counterterrorism as the cornerstone of his foreign policy, to the time of the 1986 air raid against Libya, the problem of terrorism escalated to the level of crisis. But the number of terrorist acts directed at Americans had remained relatively constant during that period, and the risk posed to Americans by terrorists was minimal. In fact, Americans were far more likely to die as a result of much more mundane events, such as crossing the street, than at the hands of a terrorist (Kupperman, 1986; Simon, 1987). Nonetheless, Americans perceived the terrorist threat to be a formidable one that required immediate government response, preferably in the form of military action. The disparity between public perception and actual magnitude of the terrorist threat invites questions about the creation of a public crisis. Why was the American public so threatened by terrorism? And how might public understanding of terrorism have helped determine the foreign policy that was endorsed?

This book attempts to answer these questions. It tells of a particular type of crisis, one that often seems remote and incomprehensible. In general, it offers a perspective from which to view the relationship between television network news and the definition, understanding, and responses to public problems. In particular, it is a book about one television news organization's presentation of international terrorism and the relationship of those news stories to the formation of foreign policy. With the growing fear of terrorism in the 1980s has come an abundance of institutional research and a proliferation of experts who offer simple explanations of television's contribution to the problem of terrorism. But little, if any, of this research has focused on the emergence of terrorism as a public problem or crisis. Part of this inattention has been due to the intensity of the national reaction and the subsequent search for immediate, short-term answers to terrorism (Morrison, 1986; Simon, 1987). Such answers have been incomplete, for it is impossible to effectively evaluate policy options without understanding the production of symbolic forms through which terrorism is represented and the knowledge that such forms reflect.

The forms on which our understanding of terrorism is based are constructed by both mass media and official discourse, or governmental rhetoric. Representations of terrorism are fundamental in understanding attitudes and behaviors toward it. "Any attempt to understand contemporary terrorism must confront the highly structured way in which news of terrorist acts, hostage reactions, government positions and rationales for positions, and public response reaches us—the audience of an ubiquitous mass mediation" (Wagner-Pacifici, 1986, p. ix). Since terrorism is not privately experienced by most Americans, public understanding must come from mass-mediated representations of terrorism and institutional reactions to it. The key to understanding the escalation of terrorism as a public problem of crisis proportions thus lies in part with the news media.

Although high-impact media portrayals of terrorism have captured the attention of communication specialists, most research remains focused on the tactics of the terrorist and the manipulation of the journalist. Terrorism, by its nature, poses a threat to established political order; news coverage of terrorist acts is seen to counteract the stabilizing function of news by conferring legitimacy to terrorists. These traditional approaches to terrorism and the media draw from a larger set of assumptions about the role of power and communication. As with other contexts in which pluralistic models of communication are appropriated, in the domain of research on terrorism and the media, such theories do not address issues of social control or attend to the role of the media in the production of consent.

Much research regarding terrorism and the media also avoids the definitional question of what constitutes terrorism. Researchers often beg the question of defining terrorism by choosing examples of it "with which few would quarrel" (Leeman, 1988). While all inquiries may not require a discussion of definitions, they are central to representations of terrorism, for they signify a power struggle over the meaning and legitimacy of political violence and domination. If terrorism, in the most general sense, is the use or threat of violence to intimidate or coerce others for political ends, then the selection of specific actions to be labeled as terrorist depends primarily on the authority of the definer. With over 100 definitions of terrorism in use (Gewen, 1987) and the evaluative nature of calling an act a terrorist one, the emergence and nature of a perceived crisis depend largely on whose definitions of terrorism prevail.

Presidents traditionally take the lead in defining crisis events for the public, and acting as a foreign policy leader often translates into presidential popularity at home. Crisis situations give presidents the opportunity to exert their role as foreign policy leaders. This role provides them "with substantially more room to maneuver and unilateral action than do other roles as economic manager or domestic policy initiator" (Marra, Ostrom and Simon, 1990, p. 591). Specific, unilateral, and dramatic action in foreign affairs can enhance the public standing of presidents if those actions are portrayed as justified and successful. As one analysis of presidential popularity demonstrates, "the public has rewarded those presidents who have taken action and have seized the center stage in the theater of foreign policy" (Marra et al., 1990, p. 520) regardless of perceived presidential ineffectiveness at home. Foreign conflicts thus provide one opportunity whereby presidents can gain political power. And, since the public acquires knowledge of foreign conflicts primarily through television news (Cohen, Adoni and Bantz, 1990), presidential popularity depends in part on how completely the news media follow the president's lead in defining foreign crisis. The role of the president in defining and orchestrating representations of terrorism is thus central to revealing the degree to which public policy and media presentations are mutually supportive.

Determinations of definitions and representations are thus necessary to understand the relationship between terrorism and the media. The process by which terrorism emerged as a public problem may be understood by addressing three concerns: (1) Who are the aggregators and transmitters of the public reality of terrorism? (2) What is the nature of that reality? (3) How does that reality influence strategies for dealing with terrorism?

The first concern (identifying the aggregators and transmitters of the public reality of terrorism) assumes that television is the primary source of public information about terrorism. During times of international crisis, Americans turn to television news, which constitutes the most widely cited source of information (Cohen, Adoni & Bantz, 1990; Larson, 1986). Television news coverage lends immediacy and visual realism to the terrorist act and adds a dimension of drama not captured in print media. Reports of terrorism presented on television constitute high drama due to the compelling nature of coverage, the centrality of personalities, the intense emotional and symbolic content, and the priestly role adopted by news personalities. Television coverage of terrorism is thus more likely to create memorable stories about terrorist events, and initial public perceptions about political violence abroad are largely based on the perspective provided by 22-minute evening newscasts. As the aggregators and transmitters of public reality, television news organizations also select the authoritative sources and expert testimony on which the credibility of the newscast relies. Information about terrorism is available from sources such as human rights groups, research institutes, foreign government officials, academics, and terrorists themselves. The sources presented by news organizations, though, come to define the terms by which terrorism is discussed. Examining the choices made in television news about which sources to consult, and thereby legitimize, will illuminate the connections between news accounts of terrorism and official policies toward it.

The second concern, the nature of the public reality of terrorism, mandates a detailed analysis of the content and form of television news accounts. Such an analysis constitutes the main focus of the research presented here. Studies of the frequency with which news media report terrorist acts and of the interdependency of terrorism and media are prevalent; however, they fail to interpret the emergent media texts about terrorism. The following study fills this gap by analyzing network news reports and determining patterns of definition and depiction in news coverage of terrorism.

Finally, the researcher who wishes to explore the relationship between media presentations and public policy formation must assess the influence of discourse about terrorism in creating the crisis of terrorism and in shaping public response to it. While any media text, print or visual, is open to a variety of interpretations, a central assumption of this analysis is that the organization and symbols of a text narrow the range of potential meanings that it is likely to generate. The answer to the third question, how the public reality of terrorism influences strategies for dealing with it, thus requires inquiry into the implications of the interpretations television news makes about acts of terrorism.

In addressing these concerns, this book gives an alternative account of the terrorist threat and public responses to it. It offers a detailed analysis of the ways in which news media support specific U.S. policy objectives rather than build sympathy for terrorists. Additionally, it traces patterns of presentation in television news that build terrorism to a problem of crisis proportions, despite both the general lack of increase in terrorist activity during the 1980s and the remoteness of danger to most U.S. citizens. Finally, this book argues that government depictions and contemporary news presentations of terrorism reproduce an ideology that supports military strength and intervention and may ultimately aid the goals of the terrorist.

The data on which this analysis is based come both from television news and government documents. President Reagan's 1981 inaugural address provides the starting point for examining the emergence of the terrorist threat. That address signaled both the release of hostages who had been held at the U.S. embassy in Tehran since November 1979 and the proclamation of counterterrorism as the new cornerstone of U.S. foreign policy. Beginning, then, with Reagan's first inaugura-tion, this study analyzes major terrorist events as presented in televised newscasts from January 1981 to April 1986, after the United States had completed its military retaliation against Libya and public attention was redirected to the unfolding Iran-Contra affair.

Televised news reports from the American Broadcasting Corporation (ABC) constitute the primary source of data for this analysis. Although a more comprehen-sive survey might include all three of the major networks, such a comparison is not necessary to address the concerns posed here.[1] Numerous studies in news formats have established consistent patterns in news presentation across the networks (see, for example, Altheide, 1982), and case studies such as Atwater's (1989) comparison of ABC, CBS, and NBC news coverage of the TWA Flight 847 hostage crisis confirm this assumption of relative consistency. Similarities exist in both content and structure. For example, Atwater (1989) concludes: "Consonance among net-works on all format criteria strongly suggests that networks shared common news values and news procedure for gathering and presenting news on the TWA incident. Network similarities appeared to go beyond message content" (p. 301).

ABC's *World News Tonight* was chosen for its extensiveness of coverage. ABC News provided the first live, international coverage of a terrorist act during its broadcast of the 1972 Munich Olympic Games, and since 1980, after the nightly airing of *The Iran Crisis: America Held Hostage*, the precursor to *Nightline*, ABC News has consistently been the top-rated newscast among the networks. ABC's emphasis on special assignments and background segments on international ter-rorism contributed to its overall coverage of terrorism during the 1980s, and ABC's total time allocated to each terrorist event surveyed here slightly exceeded that of CBS and NBC.[2]

Video reports of ABC's *World News Tonight* were obtained from the Vanderbilt Television News Archive. Attention to coverage of all terrorist acts was not necessary, for although constant references to terrorism may have contributed to a cumulative public impression about terrorists, such references do not have the impact of a major terrorist event that dominates the news for several days. Therefore, to provide focus and depth, only major terrorist acts were investigated. All terrorist events that received at least three days of consecutive coverage from each of the networks and occurred between Reagan's inauguration in January 1981 and the retaliatory bombing of Libya in April 1986 were included. These data amounted to over 12 hours, or 229 videotaped news reports acquired from the

Vanderbilt Television News Archive. The video compilations of ABC's *World News Tonight* were viewed and transcribed. The news reports were then analyzed according to the presence of key terms and their verbal and visual placement, the narrative contexts used by the networks, and the relationship of these narratives to the official discourse of the Reagan administration. In other words, this research strategy identified key terms in patterns of verbal and visual placement as they emerge in and create a public narrative of terrorism.

The strategy used here is quite different from that of traditional approaches to terrorism and media. It begins with the identification of key terms, such as the designation of an event or person as terrorist. The meaning of events and their significance for policy formation depends on their definition; words define emplotted events. Terms of deviance legitimate the power of the state by serving the dual function of both reasserting shared assumptions and values and of creating consensus by denigrating dissenters (Murdock, 1982).

Key terms also move in and out of word clusters; the context in which key terms appear can be determined by charting the patterns or word clusters in which the terms appear. The analysis of associational clusters is a process most closely identified with Kenneth Burke (1984, p. 232):

[T]he work of every writer contains a set of implicit equations. He uses "associational clusters." And you may, by examining his work, find out "what goes with what" in these clusters—what kinds of acts and images and personalities and situations go with his notions of heroism, villainy, consolation, despair, etc.

The equations of terms used in journalistic narratives is used here as an enriched approach to key terms and a way to contextualize descriptors such as "terrorist."

Key terms not only define events, but they also signal the ideology of the actor and intended audience. When terms serve to identify the social relationships and ideological commitment of a community, they can be called ideographs. As McGee (1980) explains: "The ideology of community is established by the usage of [ideographs] in specifically rhetorical discourse, for such usages constitute excuses for specific beliefs and behaviors made by those who executed the history of which they were a part" (p. 16). The polar nature of the term "terrorism" and its location in a vocabulary of political union and separation make treatment of terrorism as an ideograph particularly useful. McGee (1980) explains that an ideograph consists of a word or group of words representing ideas "understood in its relation . . . [to] other terms in its cluster" and that refer to and invoke the ideology of community (p. 14). This formulation of the ideographic vocabulary links Burke's notion of key terms within associational clusters to ideology, which McGee (1980) defines as " 'a rhetoric,' a situationally defined synchronic structure of ideograph clusters constantly reorganizing itself to accommodate specific circumstances while maintaining its fundamental consonance and unity" (p. 14). The immediate context of the term terrorism, then, is the ideographic cluster in which terrorism is verbally and visually placed.

Ideographs were also analyzed according to their placement within a journalistic narrative. Lucaites and Condit (1990, pp. 7–8) explain the essential relationship between ideographs and narratives:

Narratives are the storied forms of public discourse that extend the network of a community's vocabulary. . . . Narratives also provide the bridge to the final step by incorporating the ideal cultural values or ideographs that constitute a community. Indeed, ideographs typically function as the primary purpose term in most social narratives.

The ideographs and narratives of a group, taken together, signify the ideology of a community. Although some studies of news accounts and terrorism discuss story structure, most limit analysis of narrative to coding distinctions such as typologies of news reports according to presenter or categories of story content (see, for example, Atwater, 1989; Lule, 1988). In this analysis, the relationship between ideographs and narratives was examined. News reports were analyzed for their evaluative characterizations in the naming and describing of people and issues to uncover the process by which agents and recipients are selected and described.

In addition to the categorization of main characters and plot, narratives were analyzed according to their use of passivation, nominalization, and presupposition, and their correspondence with visual presentations. Passivation draws attention to the affected participant by placing him or her as the subject and deleting the agent of action. Instead of saying, "Hijackers are holding three American passengers on the airliner," which places the agent as subject and the affected participant as object, the statement becomes, "Three Americans are among the passengers aboard the hijacked airliner" (ABC News, March 12, 1981). Through passivation, motives or causes of action are obscured and a process is explained as the result of an attribute of the affected object (Toolan, 1988).

Nominalization, like passivation, reformulates issues of causality by transforming an implicit process "into the form of a static condition or thing" (Toolan, 1988, p. 234). Verbs are presented as noun phrases; for example, the statement, "Three gunmen demanded the release from Pakistan prisons [of] all members of the Zulfikar opposition political group," becomes, "The terrorists have now set a new deadline for the government to meet their demands" (ABC News, March 9 and 10, 1981). Nominalization is often necessary for expediency and brevity, but when words such as "terrorism," "crisis," and "demands" are transformed into nominal conditions rather than processes, audience attention is directed to the present condition (or terrorist) rather than to the underlying causes or processes that lead to terrorism. One consequence of this transformation is that, through nominalization, journalists "can report the actions of people protesting the current situation in ways that suggest that those actions—and not the situation to which they are a response—are the problem" (Toolan, 1988, p. 235). Attention to nominalization in ABC newscasts was a key means by which attributions of causality and blame were identified.

The third term, presupposition, refers to the background assumptions implicit in an utterance. Many statements in news reports seem to rely on common sense, expressed as if they were uncontroversial facts that both official sources and audiences will accept without thought. Benson (1983) suggests a similar focus in his discussion of implicit communication theory, which refers to "the collection of ideas that lay practitioners hold about the way they and others communicate"; these ideas are manifested in "instances in which understandings of key elements and processes [seem] to be implied or evoked" (pp. 104–6). Presupposition is particularly important to the study of news coverage of terrorism because over the period of five years included in this analysis, narratives about terrorism built on one another, with references to past terrorist actions and understandings about them becoming accepted as conventional wisdom.

Narratives were also analyzed according to their visual presentations. Various theorists give primacy to visual rather than verbal messages; Esslin (1982) writes that "the verbal element will of necessity either reinforce or contradict the primary message of the image to which it is subordinate. . . . It is what the characters do, not what they say, that matters in drama" (p. 20). The degree to which a verbal text supports visual images depends on characteristics such as the placement of the visual in relationship to a narrative frame and the dramatic intensity of the visual text, determined by such characteristics as the degree of movement or violence, the uniqueness of footage, the creation of discontinuity or continuity in images (as in juxtaposition or flow of images), and the mode of address used by the narrator (who is usually either seen and heard or heard offscreen). Each element was assessed for its contribution to news narratives about terrorist acts.

A final step in analysis placed the news narratives and their ideographic clusters in the discursive field of terrorism within the Reagan administration. Discursive fields create objects of discourse and determine the type of talk that will be used to discuss the object. In this view, power is more than possession of the ability to define options for others; power is "a set of pressures lodged in institutional mechanisms which *produce* and *maintain* such privileged norms" (Connolly, 1984, p. 156). The production of news embodies one such set of pressures. "News is one of the more 'closed' forms of presentation and operates almost exclusively within the terms of the official discourse" (Elliott et al., 1986, p. 269). Institutionalized media practices reproduce official discourse partly through the privileging of sources, and a survey of sources from which the network chooses reveals the way power is sustained. More significantly, the final level of analysis compares official discourse documented in the *Department of State Bulletin* and the *Weekly Compilation of Presidential Documents* with sources and material used in the ABC newscasts. The choices made by news producers at ABC impel some people to be publicly accepted as legitimate and knowledgeable authorities; these choices further the interests of some groups while minimalizing or neglecting the concerns of others.

This analysis of ideographs, narratives, and discursive fields begins only after a necessary foundation has been laid. Chapter 1 provides a brief history of the television terrorist and an overview and critique of contemporary research regarding news coverage of terrorism. Since the research on which this book is based relies on a textual approach to news, Chapter 2 provides a theoretical framework for the analysis of television newscasts. Emphasis is placed on the media role in defining deviance, the role of dramatic narratives in shaping audience interpretations of terrorism, and the process by which foreign policy problems are escalated to crisis proportions.

Chapter 3 describes the process by which characterizations of terrorists and their victims come to serve as the orientations by which journalists view unfolding terrorist events. Terrorism becomes more than a descriptor of political violence and gains currency as the ultimate enemy of U.S. national interests. The relationship of these characterizations to the narratives in which they are embedded is explored in Chapter 4, which details the use of visual referents for terrorism, the casting of top government officials as paper tigers, the formation of video postcards of hostages to mobilize viewer emotions, and the tendency to speculate about the desirability of military intervention. Chapter 5 provides an official context for these news narratives. Based on an analysis of policy statements made by White House and State Department officials, this chapter focuses on political symbols of terrorism operating in official discourse and the degree to which those symbols are legitimated in televised newscasts.

Chapter 6 extends the implications of this analysis in several ways. First, the chapter summarizes the nature of the reality of terrorism as constructed by journalists and politicians. Modifications in the idea of news framing are suggested, and standard narrative structures for television news are identified. This chapter also comments on the function of news media self-criticism in maintaining the myth of journalistic objectivity. Second, the limitations of using one network and concentrating on extended terrorist events are discussed, and directions for further research are presented. The book closes by posing a paradox. Rather than directly aiding the terrorist, television news reproduces an ideology of counterterrorism that justifies an approach to international conflict guided by symbolic gestures and overt military force. And by reinforcing and legitimizing official constructions of terrorism, television news contributes to a cycle of responses that may ultimately serve the cause of the terrorist.

In a recent article on the national security culture and terrorism, Der Derian (1989) lamented that "much of what we do know of terrorism displays a superficiality of reasoning and a corruption of language which effects truths about terrorism without any sense of how these truths are produced by and help to sustain official discourses of international relations" (p. 234). Although the analysis of media coverage of terrorism provided here does not offer a history of the social causes or grievances of terrorism or an evaluation of those grievances, it does provide an analysis of the ways in which terrorism has been publicly represented and interpreted in television network news. The focus on discourse about terrorism, or the definitions, representations, and reactions to terrorism contributes to an understanding of the relationships of act, mediation of act, audience interpretations, and subsequent reactions. Additionally, this book offers insights into the power of institutional discourse in influencing audience interpretations and public support for state repression.

Finally, most approaches to the media coverage of terrorism follow the assumptions of a contagion theory that places responsibility for the problem of terrorism on the media. The resultant solutions to terrorism are short-term media restrictions that do not address the cycle of political violence and military reaction. This analysis of the official discourse of terrorism begins to fill a critical void in revealing the forms by which terrorism is understood and the prefigured reaction to terrorism that the discourse suggests. The dimension of public crisis may further reveal how the discourse closes debate about non-military responses to terrorism and obscures a deeper distress over international disorder.

NOTES

1. Although the Cable News Network emerged as a fourth television news organization during the period considered here, its numerous format changes and lack of a comparable nightly news program made comparison of CNN with the other networks difficult. CNN has since followed the networks with *Headline News*, which seems to replicate many of the format features and content choices that characterize the networks. Nightly newscasts presented on public broadcasting stations, such as the *MacNeil Lehrer Newshour*, were excluded because they command a much smaller audience and follow a format significantly different from that used by the networks.

2. Based on information from Vanderbilt University's *Television News Index and Abstracts*, the amount of time ABC's nightly newscasts devoted to coverage of the eight major terrorist incidents used in this analysis exceeded that of CBS and NBC (ABC's coverage was 12 hours, 30 minutes; CBS, 10 hours, 52 minutes; NBC, 9 hours, 53 minutes). Weimann (1987) also notes the difference between ABC and the other two networks; during coverage of the TWA Flight 847 hijacking, "ABC devoted 68 percent of its nightly news broadcasts to the hijacking, . . . CBS dedicated 62 percent of the evening news to the TWA story, and NBC spent 63 percent of its news time covering the airline hijacking" (p. 25).

2

The Television Terrorist

Terrorism is a timeless strategy of political violence, the origins of which were discussed in ancient Greece and Rome. The act of murder for political gain has attracted many prominent advocates. For example, Cicero wrote, "As we amputate a limb in which blood and vital spirit have ceased to circulate, because it injures the rest of the body, so monsters, who, under human guise, conceal the cruelty and ferocity of a wild beast, should be severed from the common body of humanity" (*De officiis*). Discussions of tyrannicide were linked centuries later to the concept of popular sovereignty, for proponents of political assassination argued that the power of a ruler was based on a contract with his people, and if that contract was violated, sufficient grounds existed for his removal.

Tyrannicide and other forms of assassination are often placed within the domain of terrorism, but the nature of contemporary terrorism differs significantly from these tactics. Most assassinations are designed to kill a political figure for the leadership he or she provides. The tactic simulates a war maneuver, as in removing the commanding general of an army one wishes to defeat. Since at least the eighteenth century, terrorism has come to mean the systematic use of violence to coerce or intimidate a population or group. Distinction for this use of the term is commonly credited with the French, who, during the 1789 Revolution, launched a "reign of terror" to intimidate their enemies.

The strategy of terror used during the French Revolution is still some distance from our modern depictions of terrorism. But that era introduced the idea of indirect violence, of coercion through fear. Arguably, there have been social groups who, throughout history, have felt the effects of systematic terror in the form of daily oppression. Although the range of groups choosing to use terrorism as a tactic is vast, American discussions of terrorism tend to be limited (not surprisingly) to small, insurgent groups that have targeted U.S. citizens, property, or beliefs. American media also reflect this cultural predisposition. Accordingly, the following section provides a brief sketch of the evolution of contemporary terrorism, making no attempt to summarize all of the forms terrorism has taken or the various international movements in which terrorist action has played a part. Numerous volumes are devoted to this subject. Rather, the objective is to introduce to the reader prominent developments in terrorism that have influenced the orientation of U.S. media toward terrorism. With this focus, we turn to the antecedents of the television terrorists: anarchists and urban guerrillas.

THE ANTECEDENTS TO MODERN TERRORISM

The latter half of the nineteenth century was punctuated by the spread of Mikhail Bakunin's 1868 call for "propaganda by deed." This philosophy represented a shift from regarding terrorism as a strategic tactic to treating it as a symbolic act that reflected the motivations, passion, and power of a group. Bakunin's influence extended to both revolutionaries and anarchists, but the latter group was the one with which Bakunin and his student, Sergey Nechayev, allied themselves. For Bakunin, every rebellion that destabilized a government was welcomed, because the good society could only be produced by the direct annihilation of the state. His version of redemption through destruction required the participation of the masses, who could be instigated by a small group of insurrectionists carrying out a campaign of conspiratorial violence. Bakunin "offered the classical justification for heroic terrorism: attacks on the state would provoke intense, indiscriminate state repression; repression would deprive the government of legitimacy and radicalize the masses" (Rubenstein, 1987, p. 145).

Government repression was the response to a perceived anarchist bombing on May 4, 1886, in Chicago's Haymarket Square. When police charged a radical labor demonstration, an unidentified person threw a bomb into the chaotic crowd, killing several people. The ensuing execution of six Chicago anarchist leaders, convicted without evidence of their guilt (Buhle, 1987), and the resultant onset of this country's first major "red scare" effectively linked anarchism with socialism, regardless of numerous Marxist polemics against terrorism and conspiratorial violence. Associating socialists and communists with terrorism made repression of early labor movements easier, as counterterrorism tactics were used to justify mass arrests and long prison sentences (Buhle, 1987).

The Haymarket Square bombing, Alexander Berkman's attempted shooting of a Carnegie Company executive, the wave of assassination attempts on leading political figures, such as Presidents Garfield and McKinley, Spanish Prime Minister Antonio Canovas, and King Umberto of Italy, and the MacNamara brothers' bombing of the Los Angeles Times Building are a few of the events near the turn of the century that drew public attention to the use of terrorism by individuals and radical political groups. While terrorist tactics had previously focused on those who held power, they now included the taking of hostages for negotiation or ransom and the killing of innocents to attract attention to a cause. As one radical activist said, dynamite made everyone equal (Laqueur, 1987). In the United States, though most anarchists did not espouse terrorism, they became equated with the new tactic. The perception of the anarchist as "a deranged killer skulking about with a bomb hidden under his long black coat," Morgan (1989) writes, "even today colors our attitudes toward terrorism" (p. 33).

The anarchist represents both the ancestral image for the modern terrorist and a defining philosophy behind terrorism that links it to a strategy used by advocates of complete destruction. Perceived in this manner, terrorism is confined to the destabilizing activities of insurgents, and the unique challenges posed by international terrorism go unnoticed. The problem of terrorism did not receive international recognition until the assassination of King Alexander of Yugoslavia, which prompted the League of Nations to draft standards in 1937 for the prevention and punishment of terrorism. But shortly after this time, members of the League became involved in World War II, leaving India as the only country to ratify the standards. U.S. interest in terrorism subsided as well, resurfacing in the late 1950s and 1960s with the rise of the urban terrorist.

The 1960s brought two substantial changes in the nature of international terrorism. Rather than confining their activities to fighting primarily nationalistic or separatist battles in remote regions, terrorists moved to urban environments, giving them greater publicity and broader ideological appeal. At the same time, terrorists gained international support as sovereign governments began to use terrorists to fight wars by proxy or gain concessions that could not be won by traditional diplomatic or military means. And finally, the hijackings performed by Palestinian factions alerted terrorists around the world to the power of television in announcing their activities.

The last development, the use of television to amplify the effectiveness of the terrorist, is the one most relevant to the concerns raised here. Terrorists have long recognized the importance of publicity; in 1922, the British War Office described the Sinn Fein[1] mastery of publicity as unrivaled (Laqueur, 1987). Television coverage has worked best for small groups that depend most heavily on publicity, and the media provided part of the rationale for the shift from rural attacks to urban environments, where terrorists could more easily count on the audience provided by the news media. Journalists themselves were also the targets of terrorists, being threatened, abducted, or killed depending on the kind of coverage they provided (Laqueur, 1987).

Two terrorist events in the early 1970s introduced U.S. audiences to terrorism via television. On September 6, 1970, members of the Popular Front for the Liberation of Palestine (PFLP) hijacked three airliners on what came to be known as "Skyjack Sunday." The first, a TWA Boeing 707, was flying to Lebanon when hijackers diverted the plane and forced it to land on a desert airstrip in Jordan. Ten minutes after the first plane had landed, a Swissair DC-8 en route from Zurich to New York was forced to land. And a third aircraft, a Pan Am 747 leaving Amsterdam for New York, was hijacked and directed to Cairo, where the passengers were released and the aircraft destroyed.

The following day, after releasing 127 non-Israeli women and children, the PFLP held over 150 passengers and crew on the "Revolution Airstrip" in Jordan. On

September 8, a committee of nations was formed to negotiate with the hijackers and formulate a response to their demands for the release of PFLP members held in Israel, Switzerland, West Germany, and Britain. That same day, the PFLP held a press conference at Revolution Airstrip, thus exploiting the group's operation for maximum publicity.

One bargaining problem the PFLP faced was its lack of British hostages to exchange for PFLP members in Britain. On September 9, the PFLP hijacked a fourth plane, a British VC-10 carrying 116 passengers and crew. After releasing 23 of the hostages, the PFLP still held over 250 hostages at the airstrip. Conditions for the hostages worsened each day that they spent on the planes, and the hijackers became concerned about their vulnerability on the airstrip. Six days after the hijacking had commenced, the PFLP moved the passengers and crews from the aircraft and brought them into Amman. In a second television spectacle, the PFLP then staged the destruction of the three planes for the journalists and cameras.

Seventeen days and two press conferences later, all of the hostages had been released and many of the terrorists' demands had been met. The PFLP had effectively captured the world's attention and the envy of a rival Palestinian faction called Black September (O'Ballance, 1979). Following Skyjack Sunday, Black September planned and executed the second international terrorist spectacular: the Munich massacre.

The twentieth World Olympic Games opened on August 26, 1972, with nearly 5,000 journalists and television crews present. Publicity was thus guaranteed for the eight terrorists, dressed in track suits and carrying athletic bags, who stormed into a room occupied by Israeli athletes and held them hostage. The captors demanded the release of over 200 prisoners held by Israel, helicopter transportation to the Munich airport, and aircraft to fly them to an Arab capital. During subsequent negotiations, one of the terrorists, Mohammed Masalhad, appeared on the balcony wearing a hood, which provided a striking image for the many cameras focused on him. Coverage continued until the terrorists and their hostages left the housing complex; in the resulting shootings between West German authorities and the Black September terrorists, all of the Israeli athletes, five of the terrorists, and one German police officer were killed.

The Munich massacre and Skyjack Sunday were certainly not the only prominent terrorist acts in the 1970s, and terrorist action was not limited to Palestinians. Other organizations, such as the Baader-Meinhof group and the Japanese Red Army, were inspired to launch operations of their own. The two incidents detailed here are noteworthy, however, for the nature of the television coverage that they received. Terrorism in the 1970s provided the backdrop for the incident that would prompt Reagan to launch his crusade against international terrorists.

TERRORISM IN THE 1980s

U.S. attention turned once again to the Middle East in 1979, caught in the drama of the 52 hostages held at the U.S. Embassy in Tehran. The crisis began on November 4 and lasted 444 days—long enough to attempt an abortive rescue attempt, long enough to launch a late evening network news series devoted to coverage of the incident, and long enough to preoccupy and subsequently cripple a presidency. The "Iran hostage crisis" opened a new era in terrorism on television and served as a sober warning to Reagan as he took the oath of office. The hostage drama, critics argued, had paralyzed political conduct, and television had to be held accountable for creating a circus out of a crisis.

The Iran hostage crisis put the country in a state of alert regarding international terrorism. Although considerable time passed before another hostage taking incited renewed public preoccupation with terrorism, several incidents during Reagan's first term, made prominent by both journalists and public officials, served to keep terrorism in the video eye. Each of the following terrorist acts received substantial coverage in the evening newscasts of the three networks and constituted the lead news story for at least three consecutive nights. Although many other terrorist events were reported on television news during the 1980s, the ones reviewed here were the most extensive and therefore were those included for analysis.

Had it happened a decade earlier, the hijacking of a Pakistan International B-720 en route from Karachi to Peshawar probably would not have drawn substantial media attention. But in March 1981, less than three months after Reagan announced his campaign against terrorism, the incident provided the first opportunity since Reagan's inauguration to illustrate the threat posed by international terrorists. The Pakistani jet, hijacked by followers of the late Pakistani Prime Minister Zulfikar Ali Bhutto, carried 145 passengers; several of them were U.S. citizens. The hijackers' demands included instructions for coverage of the incident on Pakistani radio and the release of political prisoners held in Pakistani jails. By March 14, the Pakistani government had released several prisoners and paid a $50,000 ransom to the hijackers. The plane had by this time been flown to Syria, where the terrorists surrendered and the hostages were released. The incident was primarily an internal one for Pakistan and was deemed international only due to the presence of foreign nationals on the plane.

The only major terrorist event during Reagan's first term that did not take place in the Middle East was the abduction of Brigadier General James Dozier on December 17, 1981. Dozier was kidnapped in his home by members of the Red Brigades who posed as plumbers and who called for a war against NATO and "the American military machine" (Mickolus et al., 1989). Several communiques from the Red Brigades followed, one including a picture of Dozier. Several police arrests and investigations later, Italian authorities raided the apartment in which Dozier was being held. After 42 days in captivity, Dozier was freed.

Nearly two years passed before terrorism was again a preoccupation with U.S. networks. Sporadic bombings and hijackings had certainly occurred; for instance, in August 1982, a passenger was killed when a bomb exploded on a Pan Am jet headed for Honolulu. But none of these events received extended media coverage. The next terrorist incident to capture public attention came on October 23, 1983, when a suicide bomber drove a yellow Mercedes truck filled with TNT into a housing complex for U.S. Marines stationed at Beirut International Airport. The explosion killed 241 U.S. service members and injured 80 others. Seconds later, another terrorist drove a car loaded with explosives into an apartment in which 110 French paratroopers were housed. The blast destroyed the building, killing 58 of the military personnel and injuring at least 15 more. The Islamic Jihad claimed responsibility for the bombings, saying that the action was in retaliation for the presence of foreign military forces in Lebanon.

This event dominated evening newscasts for two nights, before it was overshadowed by the U.S. invasion of Grenada on October 25. Coverage of the Beirut bombing was extensive, though, and the bombing and the invasion were linked both in television news accounts and official public statements. For several months following the bombings, public interest in terrorism seemed to wane, as the next extended terrorist event on U.S. television was not broadcast until the summer of 1985. On June 14, TWA Flight 847, carrying 145 passengers and eight crew members, left Athens and headed for Boston via Rome. Ten minutes after taking off, two Lebanese passengers armed with a pistol and hand grenades stormed the cockpit and ordered the captain, John Testrake, to fly to Beirut. After initially denying landing rights, Lebanese officials allowed the plane to land. The events that followed came to constitute America's second hostage crisis.

The hijackers released 17 women and two children and demanded that the plane be flown to Algiers and then back to Beirut. On landing in Beirut the second time, one of the hijackers beat and fatally shot Robert Stethem, who had not lowered his head quickly enough to satisfy the hijacker. His body was thrown on the tarmac, and more gunmen boarded the plane. They removed four passengers with Jewish-sounding names before flying back to Algiers on June 15. There, Algerian officials boarded the plane and received a set of demands from the hijackers, which included the exchange of Greek hostages for a terrorist held in Greece, the release of Arabs in Israeli prisons, and the withdrawal of Israeli troops from Lebanon. Before leaving Algiers to return to Beirut, the hijackers had won the release of Ali Atwah, the terrorist held in Greece, and had released all but 44 of the passengers on the plane.

Several developments occurred over the next two weeks. Shi'ite leader Nabih Berri assumed the role of negotiator for the hijackers, more hostages were released, and though the crew remained on board the plane, the passengers were separated into groups and moved to West Beirut. ABC News correspondents were allowed to interview the crew while they spoke from the cockpit, Berri held press conferences with the hostages, and ABC journalists and hostages ate together in a staged (and heavily guarded) meal before television cameras. On June 30, all remaining hostages from TWA Flight 847 were released. The second hostage crisis was over, but it had renewed criticisms and raised many questions about the relationship between television and terrorists.

A spate of terrorist events that fall and in the spring of 1986 prefaced the U.S. strike against Libya. On October 7, four gunmen took control of the *Achille Lauro*, an Italian cruise ship. The hijacking of the ship constituted a crime against Italy, but 12 of the 97 passengers were U.S. tourists. On orders from the terrorists, Captain

Gerardo de Rosa headed for Syria, which denied permission to dock. The hijackers demanded the release of Palestinian terrorists held by Israel, and as negotiations proceeded, the hijackers became impatient. They singled out Leon Klinghoffer, a 69-year-old New Yorker in a wheelchair who had suffered two strokes, and shot him in the head and chest. The hijackers then ordered two crew members to throw Klinghoffer's body overboard.

After receiving a message later determined to have been from Abu Abbas, a Palestinian Liberation Front leader, the hijackers ordered the ship to head back to Port Said. By October 9, the terrorists were communicating with Egyptian officials and with Abbas. Later that evening, the hijackers left the ship under the escort of Egyptian authorities and Abbas. Egypt denied the U.S. request to turn the hijackers over to them, and Egyptian President Hosni Mubarak claimed that the hijackers had already left the country. They hadn't. The U.S. National Security Agency had eavesdropped on the conversations of Egyptian officials, and agents knew that the hijackers were aboard a chartered Egypt Air 737, waiting to be flown to Tunisia. Using Navy F-14s, U.S. pilots intercepted the Egyptian aircraft and forced it to land at a U.S.–Italian air base in Sicily. Although the U.S. commandos wanted custody of the four hijackers, the Italians had jurisdiction over them and arrested them. More importantly, the Reagan administration wanted Abbas to stand trial for the hijacking, but the Italians allowed Abbas to flee only two days later.

The victimization of U.S. travelers during 1985 ended with the December 27 massacres at the El Al ticket counters of the Rome and Vienna airports. Twenty people, five of them Americans, were killed when terrorists threw hand grenades and opened fire with Kalashnikov automatic rifles in two attacks timed within 15 minutes of each other. Although the incident was short-lived and not staged for media attention, subsequent investigations to determine the group or leader responsible for the massacre received considerable coverage. Similarly, when a bomb exploded on TWA Flight 840 on April 2, 1985, causing the death of four passengers, media attention turned to speculations about the organization responsible for the bombing. Three days later, a bomb exploded in the washroom of the LaBelle discotheque in West Berlin, killing three people and wounding 231 others. The two events and their investigations and reactions constituted a consistent focus in television news that ended with the April 15, 1986, bombing of Libya by the United States.

The air raid against Libya gave the United States an opportunity to exercise military power against terrorism, but it could not free the remaining hostages in Lebanon. Reagan's efforts to bargain with terrorists marred the end of his presidency. Although he had begun his tenure with strong statements about a no-concessions policy and swift and effective retribution for terrorism, he completed it with an arms-for-hostages scandal that damaged the credibility of his calls for counterterrorism. Consumed with the Iran-Contra affair, television cameras turned from terrorism. But the implications of the coverage that television had provided throughout the 1980s remained the focus of much scholarship and debate.

TERRORISM AND MEDIA INTERDEPENDENCE:
CONTAGION THEORY

Terrorism is caused by factors too numerous to detail here. Television, however, does not constitute one of those factors; it is not a direct cause of terrorism. But since the mid-1970s, most discussions about the relationship of terrorism and media have proceeded on the assumption that news coverage encourages the spread of terrorism. Using Clutterbuck's (1975) oft-quoted passage—"The television camera is like a weapon lying in the street. Either side can pick it up and use it" (p. 147)—subscribers to the contagion theory argue that the media are instruments used by terrorists to create a theater of terror, commanding publicity, gaining a following, and spreading information about terrorist tactics. Terrorists use the media as a "loudspeaker" (Gal-Or, 1985) to draw attention to their tactics and causes (Alexander & O'Day, 1984; Dowling, 1986; Gal-Or, 1985; Laqueur, 1987). A statement made by the American Legal Foundation is representative of those who support the contagion theory: "Because they give the terrorists a convenient stage to vent their political grievances, the media actually encourage terrorism and may promote the increasing violence and drama of terrorist acts" (in Picard, 1990, p. 316). Lacking media coverage, contagion theorists argue, terrorists would have no visibility or hope of legitimacy, and thus terrorism would be reduced.

The contagion theory informs much conventional wisdom about terrorism and the media. According to the theory, news media serve the terrorist in three fundamental ways: by providing exposure to a public, by conferring legitimacy on the terrorist's cause, and by supplying information about tactics and strategies to other terrorists. Each of these claims and the implications of contagion theory for media policy will be discussed.

Yonah Alexander (1979), a leading proponent of the contagion theory, cites the attention drawn to the terrorist by extensive media coverage as a primary reward for the terrorist. He compares terrorism to advertising and claims that the effectiveness of the terrorists' message is increased "by focusing on spectacular incidents and by keeping particular incidents alive through repetition" (p. 333). Attention to terrorism not only keeps the issue alive in the public mind as an ever-present threat but also, according to Alexander and O'Day (1984), amounts to greater support for the terrorist's cause. They explain that "by providing extensive coverage of incidents the media give the impression that they sympathize with the terrorist cause, thereby creating a climate congenial to further violence" (p. 146).

Public exposure of terrorist acts in media coverage is thus posed as tantamount to legitimacy for the terrorist. Not only does access to the media legitimate the terrorist, but, contagion theorists state, the press often portrays terrorist causes in a sympathetic manner. Journalists exculpate terrorism, Merari and Friedland (1985) write, and they act as allies to the terrorist by criticizing public officials. Netanyahu (1986) claims that the "world's free press assists the terrorists" because it "often adopts their terminology and arguments and transmits them to the public uncritically, even sympathetically" (p. 109). Although not all supporters of the contagion theory emphasize press bias in their account of the ways in which media coverage helps encourage terrorism (e.g., Gal-Or, 1985; Livingstone, 1986), the claim that coverage enhances the legitimacy of the terrorist is central to the contagion theory.

A final assumption of the contagion theory is that media coverage supplies information about the methods of terrorists as well as their political objectives and rationales. As terrorists watch other terrorists on television, they learn from each other. "The exportation of violent techniques ... in turn often triggers similar extreme actions by other individuals and groups" (Alexander & O'Day, 1984, p. 139). Watching a successful terrorist attack may increase the morale of other terrorists (Dowling, 1986) and "may advance not only further acts of terrorism, but also the adoption of terrorist tactics by common criminals" (Gal-Or, 1985, p. 18).

This emphasis on the importance of media coverage for the success of terrorism places primary responsibility for curbing terrorism on the news media, for "without the assistance of the modern media, terrorism would probably be significantly reduced" (Gal-Or, 1985, p. 15). Most scholars who rely on the contagion theory make normative statements about how or if the media should cover terrorism; for example, Bassiouni's work (1982) includes policy perspectives that emerge from the assumptions of the contagion theory. Bassiouni notes the double-edged reliance by both governments and the public on the media as a source of information, and the subsequent legitimacy media coverage may confer on terrorists. The choice by the terrorist of acts with psychological impact "contribute[s] to the newsworthiness of certain acts that are intrinsically common crimes, whose harmful effect is of very limited significance in comparison to other crimes" (Bassiouni, 1982, p. 129). Because of the conflicts, ranging from journalists aiding the terrorists to escalating violence, Bassiouni argues for the adoption of voluntary guidelines by the media. He offers a set of prescriptions by which the press can help delegitimize terrorism (Bassiouni, 1982, p. 141):

Clearly judgments must be made by journalists that differentiate between wars of ideas fought within legitimated institutions of the community, and struggles fought outside these institutions and which rely upon violence rather than verbiage, intimidation rather than intellect.

Other contagion theorists agree that the amount and type of coverage need to be restricted. Gal-Or (1985) argues that terrorist acts "should be condemned and subject to contempt by the media" (p. 45).

Contagion theorists, in their assumptions and prescriptions, begin and end with a pragmatic view of media as instruments to be used for good or evil. But this approach and the subsequent claims about the degree to which news coverage creates terrorism are problematic and deserve scrutiny. Picard (1990) summarizes his criticisms of the contagion theory by pointing to the absence of research to validate it: "No single study based on accepted social science research methods has established a cause–effect relationship between media coverage and the spread of terrorism" (p. 315). The validity of Picard's indictment can be assessed by questioning the contagion theory's assumptions of the increased visibility, legitimacy, and spread of information that are granted to the terrorist through media coverage.

Although terrorists do gain publicity from news coverage, the effects of this coverage are less clear. Contagion research that looks at actual instances of news coverage is rare, but one such study does demonstrate a relationship of escalation between terrorists and the media. Drawing from his content analysis of selected newspaper reports of the Irish Republican Army (IRA) over a 70-year period, Tan (1988) found that "the amount of publicity terrorists receive is an important predictor of the subsequent level of terrorist violence" (p. 18). He explains this relationship not as one of increased legitimacy, morale, or tactical information for the terrorist but as an escalation imperative by which already involved terrorists in an ongoing conflict "escalate the scale of violence by employing higher-powered explosives, for example, rather than recruiting more perpetrators" (p. 18). This more intensified violence "might explain why the audience usually perceives that there is more terrorist violence today than yesterday, where there is actually less violence" (Tan, 1988, p. 22). The desire to gain media attention, Tan argues, contributes to an escalation effect rather than a contagion effect.

Tan's study emphasizes the terrorist's attraction to publicity without supporting the contagion view of increased legitimacy for the terrorist. Evidence of legitimacy conferred through coverage is, as yet, nonexistent. Alexander (1979), for example, uses public opinion polls about audience awareness of the Palestine Liberation Organization (PLO) to support the inference that awareness of terrorist acts amounts to support for the group. But as Schlesinger (1981) counters, "Public recognition of a group's existence does not indicate that its goals are now publicly favored. Nor, indeed, does recognition mean that the public necessarily understands the political aims of the group in question in terms that it itself would wish" (p. 88; see also Picard, 1990). Legitimacy in the form of enhanced morale for other terrorists also remains unsupported. While Dowling (1986) suggests that such an effect may exist, no study of terrorist groups exists to support this claim.

Finally, no empirical research exists to demonstrate a sympathetic slant in reporting about terrorism. In their analysis of the *New York Times* and the *Times* of London, Kelly and Mitchell (1984) found news reports to be "sapping terrorism of its political content" by "focusing on the sensational aspects of the incident" rather than providing explanations about it. Terrorists do not receive coverage about their political motivations; "less than 10 percent of the coverage in either newspaper dealt in even the most superficial way with the grievances of the terrorists" (p. 287). As Gerbner (1988) argues, it may not be the terrorist who receives legitimacy from coverage; rather, "the media, placed in a position to report the facts of the terrorist situation, receives enhanced credibility" (p. 1). Additionally, press bias tends to run in favor of official stands against terrorism. Schlesinger (1981) summarizes that "the orthodox view of the media as 'willing victims' of the terrorists . . . fails to attend to how the media routinely deny the rationality of anti-state political violence and how in some circumstances they invoke the sacred dimension of nationhood to ward off subversive evil" (p. 96).

Schlesinger's and Gerbner's claims deserve further empirical support. At this point, though, one can conclude that the assumption that media coverage alone spreads terrorism is simplistic and unsupported: "To argue that the presence of the media alone explains the taking of a terrorist action is simplistic reductionism that treats media as unrealistically divine, and political terrorism as undoubtedly non-ideological or pathological" (Tan, n.d., p. 18). The media may contribute to the spread of terrorism, but only when there are other, direct causes.

Direct causes of terrorism include the ease of international travel, the availability of weapons and financial support, and the relatively minimal risk of terrorist warfare in a nuclear age. This latter issue of minimal risk becomes manifest in at least two ways. First, nations with nuclear capability have been unwilling, thus far, to engage in open warfare that could escalate; covert or proxy wars fought by guerrillas or mercenaries using terrorist tactics have become a means by which states can exert influence in other countries without risking the potential escalation of conventional war. Second, terrorism is fairly cheap and simple, and small, disenfranchised groups can achieve significant damage with minimal risk of apprehension or retribution. Finally, the view that terrorism is spread primarily through media coverage promulgates the contagion theory as conventional wisdom and thus shifts attention from the nature of news coverage and politically motivated violence to issues of press censorship.

TELEVISION COVERAGE AND PUBLIC PERCEPTION

The impact of media coverage on public perceptions of terrorism has been approached in a variety of ways, ranging from content analyses of news coverage to conceptualizations of terrorism as rhetoric. Much of this research explores the interdependence of terrorism and the media, but the emphasis of these studies shifts from issues of media encouragement to the nature of media representations of terrorism.

The impact of media coverage on public understanding of terrorism is emphasized in Weimann's (1983) experimental study. To demonstrate the "important role [of coverage] in the process of image formation or in the definition of a situation, especially when they are relied upon heavily for information" (p. 39), Weimann showed a group of undergraduates press clippings describing terrorist events and used semantic differential scales to evaluate the students' changes in attitudes about terrorists. Weimann found that exposure to press coverage increased agreement among students that: the problem that caused the terrorist act is important; the problem should have been covered by the media and solved by international institutions; people should know about the problem; and the respondent would like to know more about the subject. Weimann (1983, p. 44) concludes:

Press attention appears to be sufficient to enhance the status of the people, problem, or cause behind a terrorist event. Terrorists' success in attracting media attention may then guarantee worldwide awareness and recognition of the political, racial, or religious problem that caused the event.

This demonstration of status conferral based on newspaper representations may seem to confirm contagion theory assumptions. Limitations of Weimann's study, however, do not warrant such conclusions. Perhaps most importantly, the generic "problem" that respondents deem important is never specified. Further, any experimental situation, but especially one involving Israeli undergraduates living in the midst of political violence and terrorism, may spark curiosity among respondents about the subject of the study. Finally, the structure of news reports may cumulatively delegitimize contextual issues of terrorism. At the least, though, Weimann (1983) has helped demonstrate that the lack of preestablished attitudes about terrorism and audience dependency on the media for information increase the impact of news coverage.

Knight and Dean's (1982) analysis of Canadian news coverage of the 1980 seizure of the Iranian Embassy in London deals more directly with the relationship between public perception and media treatment of a terrorist act. Drawing on several studies that show how the structure of news helps define public reality, Knight and Dean apply the concept of myth to show that news reports legitimize the use of state violence as a response to terrorism. The authors focus on mythic themes of mystery and legitimacy of the Special Air Services (SAS) regiment of the British army, the men who recaptured the embassy. As such, the study is limited, for few terrorist acts result in military intervention. As an analysis of institutional response, though, the study advances the idea of the "dependent instrumentalism" of the SAS and its actions. SAS violence is "legitimated so long as it *responds* to the illicit violence—'terrorism'—initiated by those who disrupt social order," whereas the Iranian gunmen, portrayed without a context beyond that of their violent tactics, become assimilated "into the myth of Iran-as-bad-news" (p. 59).

Mythic themes also provide a framework for Lule's (1988) analysis of *New York Times* coverage of the *Achille Lauro* hijacking. Based on a dramatistic approach to two weeks of news accounts, Lule argues that the widow of Leon Klinghoffer, who was killed during the incident, became the focal point within an emergent myth of the "innocent victim sacrificed." Like Knight and Dean (1982), Lule (1988) notes the importance of news contextualization for locating the terrorist act within a symbolic narrative. In Lule's analysis, the myth is one in which the victim is transformed into an international hero and political symbol. This myth promotes audience identification of the reader with the victim and may help to foster the terror of terrorism (Lule, 1988). Conclusions about the extent to which news coverage uses this myth of the victim to contextualize terrorist acts must remain tentative; as Lule states, the *New York Times* is the "hometown" paper of the Klinghoffers and could be expected to emphasize the local angle of this particular incident. But the possibilities for audience identification with the mythic victim are clear, and Lule's analysis provides direction for further analysis of the forms by which the terror of terrorism is intensified through news accounts.

Additional studies of terrorism have focused on themes of audience identification and the rhetorical forms of terrorism. Some of this research focuses on a distinction between (1) mass, "public," and (2) "peer" audiences, or other terrorists. For example, Dowling (1986) argues that the "terrorist spectacular" contains recurring forms of "strategic responses to the situational restraints and purposes of the rhetors" that classify some terrorist activities as a rhetorical genre. In explaining the terrorist's need to incite repressive government reactions and the constraints posed by using news media as vehicles of expression, Dowling (1986) gives one of the clearer formulations of the interrelationship between media and terrorism. Although he distinguishes between two audiences of terrorism, insiders and outsiders, his discussion of messages to insiders (other terrorists) does not go beyond the point that terrorist acts may increase the morale of other terrorists.

Like Dowling (1986), Leeman (1987) combines a focus on inside audiences with an understanding of terrorism as rhetoric and assesses the political implications of this combination. By looking at official reactions to *perceived* messages to other terrorists, Leeman recasts the rhetorical approach to the insider/outsider distinction and minimizes the necessity for data from terrorists. Leeman (1987) argues that terrorism serves an epideictic function for the terrorist because the act demonstrates commitment to a set of values that challenges existing authority and justifies terrorism: "Terroristic violence *implies* an epideictic facet even if the terrorist does not mean it to" (p. 51). He then turns (1987, p. 52) to the "responding rhetor," the official response, and explains the relationship between terrorist act and reaction:

The responding rhetor can plausibly read into the violence a rhetoric threatening the value system. . . . This symbolic challenge to the symbol makes coherent Reagan's justification for sanctions on Libya: because of an "unusual and extraordinary threat to the national security and foreign policy of the U.S." Such a rhetorical response may not be accurate, but it is coherent given the epideictic challenge to our system.

Leeman moves discussion of rhetorical forms to the level of official response and privileges this form of rhetoric rather than the more elusive effect of the terrorist act on other terrorists. His approach adds depth to our understanding of the rhetorical dimensions of terrorist violence, but Leeman stops short of extending his analysis to public perceptions of official responses to terrorism as presented in the news media.

A useful extension of a focus on the rhetoric of response comes from Palmerton's (1988) analysis of CBS coverage of the 1979-80 Iranian hostage crisis. She begins with the premise that, for Americans, "the meaning of terrorism is shaped in large part by the major vehicle we use to gain our primary information about events occurring outside our immediate circle of experience: the news media" (p. 106). Consistent with previous research, Palmerton (1988) states that terrorists use news media to reach their target audience. Additionally, she argues that rhetorical impact for the terrorist is achieved through responses to the terrorist act: "*It is the response which becomes the primary persuasive vehicle for the terrorist*" (p. 107). Several scholars have explained terrorism as a strategy aimed at inciting repressive government response, thereby shifting the terrorist to the role of victim and/or escalating a cycle of retaliation (e.g., Dowling, 1986; Rubenstein, 1987; Schmid & deGraaf, 1982; Simon, 1987). Palmerton's work suggests that the rhetoric generated in response to mass-mediated terrorism may help the terrorist's strategy.

Thus, one way in which the terrorist's aims are furthered is by upsetting the public's conviction that its government is justified in taking repressive measures against terrorists. But the likelihood of an audience questioning the legitimacy of government retaliation depends largely on the manner in which this audience learns about official reactions. The rhetoric of response more likely aids in the building of consensus for government counterterrorism strategies. Gerbner (1988, p.1) explains that while

perpetrators of small-scale acts of violence and terror may occasionally force media attention and, in that sense, seem to advance their cause, in the last analysis such a challenge . . . is used to mobilize support for repression often in the form of wholesale state violence and terror or military action, presented as justified by the provocation.

In this view, state power is legitimated and enhanced through media coverage of terrorism. Such legitimation is necessary to gain public consent for repressive measures, for as the state exercises increasing levels of control, the media play a much more crucial role in winning consent for increasingly coercive policies.

The roles of the media in contributing to a cycle of repression and violence and in framing events through news accounts are thus interrelated processes. Challenging public confidence, like persuading audiences to sympathize with terrorists, depends largely on the nature of the news accounts that tell viewers how to understand unfolding events. One of the more thorough treatments of news narratives about terrorism has come from Brown (1990), who contends that hijackers of TWA Flight 847, through Shi'ite leader Nabih Berri's rhetoric as presented in ABC *World News Tonight*, *Good Morning America*, *Time*, *Newsweek*, and *U.S. News and World Report*, persuaded the U.S. public to accept the legitimacy of the hijackers' demands. But though the public may have voiced support of U.S. compromises to obtain the hostages' release, this position did not require an understanding of the larger political aims of the terrorists or granting the terrorists legitimacy. Prior research suggests that television news provides neither type of information (Gerbner, 1988; Kelly & Mitchell, 1984; Schlesinger, 1981; Picard, 1990). Additionally, Brown focused on the narrative advanced by an actor—Berri—in the terrorist drama, rather than the narrative context in which Berri's comments were embedded. Finally, Brown combined news media that rely on varied narrative formats. The equivocation of news structure in news magazine feature stories with that of nightly television newscasts prevented a detailed examination of the narrative form prevalent in either source.

By focusing on patterns of dramatic structure in television narratives, this analysis illuminates the relationship between the form and function of news stories about terrorism.

CONCLUSION

The use of terrorism as a strategy of political violence is ancient, but the perceived emergence of terrorism as a problem of crisis proportions represents a relatively new problem caused in part by television. The influence of television has prompted several questions about relationships among terrorists, media, and foreign policy. Contemporary research investigating these relationships has relied largely on the contagion theory, a simple and reductionistic model that lacks substantial evidence of the actual use of media by terrorists. A second strand of research explores public perceptions of terrorism and emphasizes the rhetorical effect of terrorism, particularly in influencing official responses to terrorist acts. Most of this research, however, ignores the institutional power derived from responding to terrorism and the degree to which the dominant ideology is reflected and reconstructed in news coverage of terrorism. Research regarding news coverage of terrorism, like other analyses of news accounts, needs to address the process by which consent is formed. To do this

we need to make the analytical separation between the discourses the media produce and the discourses they use as material to build on, process, and deliver. We need to be interested in the structures of transformation. We cannot ignore—as most content analysis does—the discursive components from which reports are constructed. (Bruck, 1989, p. 117)

The following analysis examines the process by and the materials from which representations of terrorism are constructed to illuminate the relationship among terrorist acts, media coverage, and the production of consent.

NOTE

1. Sinn Fein is the political wing of the Irish Republican Army.

3

The Interpretation of Television News

Privileging television news as the primary source of public knowledge about terrorism would be useless without a firm understanding of the news reporting process and its influence on public opinion and behavior. Many discussions of television news and terrorism start with the assumption that news coverage benefits the terrorist, but it is important to note that this premise ignores the structural attributes of news and the contributions they make to the public's understanding of terrorism. News stories are organized according to standard production formulas; television audiences need not only to be informed but also seduced, entertained, and in the proper state of mind for advertisers. News stories are also based on the intuitive, professional assumptions of news journalists and producers. These characteristics of news help determine the telling of the news stories and the way in which audiences are likely to interpret them.

In their attempt to make sense of the world in a seemingly objective manner, journalists must organize events according to the practices that media institutions require them to adopt. To handle the flow of unexpected events, journalists rely on frames, or categories of perception. Gitlin (1980) notes the importance of media frames as "largely unspoken and unacknowledged" patterns of presentation and interpretation that "organize the world both for journalists who report it and, in some important degree, for us who rely on their reports" (p. 7). The journalistic standards that inform these frames arise from the process of selecting and shaping stories. These structurally and institutionally imposed frames fit social conventions and basic assumptions about the formation of U.S. foreign policy. Journalists can be expected to present "a particular type of news, not because they feel obliged to do so, but rather because they feel this is the type of news that is appropriate for the American public to read" (Epstein, 1977, p. 75).

Press perceptions of the audience also determine the extent to which government policies will be criticized. In general, news frames can be expected to support corporate capitalism (Gitlin, 1980); journalists will challenge the prevailing political norm only with an attentive audience that is similarly willing to scrutinize government policies (Tan, 1989).

The influence of news frames in coverage of international terrorism has received moderate attention from researchers. One such study comes from Carpini and Williams (1984). In their comparison of television network coverage of terrorism from 1969 to 1980, Carpini and Williams found that news conventions contribute to a distorted picture that exaggerates terrorist incidents in the Middle East, deemphasizes terrorism in Latin America, stresses government victimization, and ignores terrorist actions against corporations. They conclude that "none [of the networks' coverage] very closely parallels the patterns of actual occurrence of international terrorism," and they explain these inaccuracies as consequences of the manner by which news reports are gathered and of the journalists' acceptance of what Gans (1979) calls the "enduring values" of "altruistic democracy, ethnocentrism, and an abiding faith in social order" (Carpini & Williams, 1984, pp. 108–119). Similar findings have been reported for print as well as broadcast media. For instance, Fuller (1988) surveyed coverage of terrorism in the *Christian Science Monitor* between 1977–87 and found that reports of terrorism increased fivefold from 1984 to 1985. For the years from 1981–87, the least attention to terrorism was given in 1984, when, by the *Monitor*'s own news accounts, the number of terrorist incidents was at its highest. The amount of attention to terrorism given by news organizations depends less on the frequency of terrorist acts than on the frames that are used to decide which events merit coverage.

Research that establishes the lack of a necessary correspondence between patterns of terrorist activity and the frequency with which events are reported runs counter to official perspectives about the relationship between terrorism and the media. As Frank Perez (1984), deputy director of the Office for Combatting Terrorism with the U.S. Department of State proclaims, "the United States press seems to be mostly event-oriented. Every terrorist event which occurs is reported" (p. 19). Not only do many terrorist events go unreported, but those that are covered by news media fit institutional frames developed largely on the basis of the news organization's relationships with public figures and official institutions. As Epstein (1977) notes in his analysis of news coverage of terrorism in Latin America, the dependency of correspondents on official sources creates a need for the media to follow the lead of government, and makes them "hesitant to write articles opposed to United States government policy for fear of being excluded from future tips or special briefings" (p. 12; see also Gans, 1979).

The role of news media in choosing which events to report is often called the agenda-setting function of the media. According to Shaw and McCombs (1971), agenda setting refers to the strong relationship between the emphasis of topics in the news media and the salience of these topics to the public. But news media also create salient topics for politicians. As Graber (1989) explains: "Media coverage is the very lifeblood of politics because it shapes the perceptions that form the reality on which political action is based" (p. 238). As news media define political environments and politicians respond to public opinion as it is portrayed on television, the direction of influence between politicians and journalists becomes reciprocal rather than unidirectional. News media, then, both reflect the institutional frames of perception provided by government officials and further define situations for both public and political audiences.

SEMIOTIC APPROACHES TO NEWS

Although the process by which news frames are formed may help explain the types of stories and representations that are selected by journalists, the analysis of representations of terrorism as media texts requires an interpretive approach to news reports. News frames are critical in the selection of events to be covered, but they play a limited role in the transformation of the event into a news story. For the purposes of understanding media representations of terrorism, semiotics can provide a focus on verbal and visual linguistic techniques of depiction in the creation of consensus.

Semiotic analyses of news often begin with a discussion of encoding, or transforming event into story. For an event to become a story, it must be signified within the rules of verbal and visual language. As Hall (1980) writes, "The event must become a 'story' before it can become a communicative event" (p. 129). Research in terrorism and news coverage that proceeds on this assumption of encoding often explores the semantic dimension of terrorism to see how media discourse reproduces dominant meanings (Schlesinger, 1981). For example, Epstein (1977) looks at the labeling of terrorism in its transformation from event to story; the use of political labeling is "one of the most common means of creating approval for particular aspects of [U.S. foreign] policy" (p. 67). Like Epstein, Weimann has also looked at the labeling of terrorism by the press. Based on a content analysis of Israeli press coverage of terrorism, Weimann (1985) argues that a trend exists to label politically remote terrorist organizations in positive terms. This trend may have a significant impact on public opinion because of public dependency on the media for information about terrorism and because of the lack of preconceived attitudes toward politically remote terrorist organizations.

The encoding of event into story places constraints on the types of interpretations audiences are likely to make about terrorism. Events are transformed into stories based on the common images of a culture, and as those images are appropriated, they also shape the range of understandings about the event. Patterns of presentation can thus provide the boundary conditions, or limits, of interpretation. Approaching news as providing ideological closure in this manner runs counter to claims of audience use or open interpretation of media messages, and assumes that the text places constraints on interpretations. Lewis (1985, p. 210) explains:

The viewer will, on the whole, have only a limited range of appropriate meaning systems (extra-textual contexts) to draw upon when watching a television news story. These contexts will give the viewer a specific form of access to certain sections (lexias) of the item, which will, in turn, force him/her towards a certain meaning (or set of meanings).

The common images and cultural norms created in the media also indirectly influence conduct. In matters of public policy, these norms "act to build or to reinforce public support for decisions made by a limited group of policy-makers in government. The press plays a most essential role in conditioning the public to accept such policy without serious discussion of either its implications or its alternatives" (Epstein, 1977, p. 76; see also Ettema & Glasser, 1988). Similarly, Gerbner (1988) argues that the real victim in the process of labeling terrorists is "a community's ability to think rationally and creatively about injustice" (p. 1). The process of defining and labeling terrorists is central to representations of terrorism and can be explored in the encoding of terrorist events in news accounts.

THE STRUCTURE OF NEWS STORIES

Definitions and labels reach publics through the narratives in which they are located. The reporting process itself has been called a "literary act, a continuous search for 'story lines' that goes so far as to incorporate the metaphors and plots of novels, folk traditions, and myths" (Nimmo & Combs, 1985, p. 16). Like the novelist, the journalist makes events intelligible by placing them in a narrative structure that allows the journalist to tell a story. Some of the structural elements of the news story have been explored for their reliance on news frames, as identified earlier. An additional constraint of news narratives exists at an ideological level, for news media must "typically espouse some variant or other of the dominant ideology of the community of potential readers, and have to engage in this espousal (or articulation or legitimation) even in the course of reporting news that is 'awkward' for that ideology." Thus, the " 'background' narrative of how the world is" prevails over the incongruities of individual stories (Toolan, 1988, p. 228).

At the broadest level, then, background narratives tell the journalist how to report a story according to institutional conventions. The drama of terrorism is told within the narrative of the news theme, a unifying concept that frames definitions of news events. The news theme allows journalists to present a specific event or series of events as an example of some broader concept. At a more specific level, narrative contexts for individual news stories provide "a particular history that gives a news item (or parts of that item) meaning" (Lewis, 1985, p. 205). The relationship of the news story as narrative to the production of meaning is usually approached as an evaluation of the correspondence of the story to some external reality, an application of narrative to identify story structure for expediency in coding content, or, least common, as an analysis of the structural constraints the televisual narrative places on audience interpretation of an event. This last approach is the one developed here.

Few researchers still support the idea that there is a transparent correspondence between actual events and news reports of them. Rather, news stories reorder events and provide the means by which the moral significance of an event can be judged.

Fisher calls news accounts "real fictions," because although stories are based on actual events, they cannot be empirically verified in detail. Nimmo and Combs (1985) summarize Fisher's argument: The world portrayed on television news "is a dramatic pseudo-reality created from an ongoing flow of happenings 'out there' but transformed into an entertaining story that conforms to the logic of the medium while assisting people to relate those events to their everyday lives" (p. 16). Thus, although the news story is based on actual events, it is bound by the narrative structure that contains it. And news stories are meaningful not just because of their intrinsic structural relationships but because of the degree to which audiences identify with stories. Narratives are a social transaction, linking speaker and audience; this linkage is performed through specific forms that create expectations and resonate with audiences.

Thus, even though news narratives are based on actual events, they are necessarily subjective. Newscasts provide stories about reality, and because they draw from real rather than fictional happenings, they are more seductive in their power to influence. We treat news accounts as a chronicle or report rather than a story. As Hall (1984) laments, "We make an absolutely too simple and false distinction between narratives about the real and narratives of fiction" (p. 6), when the forms of both types of narratives are essentially the same. He elevates the status of form, for it activates meaning: "Meanings are already concealed or held within the forms of the stories themselves. Form is much more important than the old distinction between form and content" (1984, p. 7). This emphasis on form extends White's (1981) analysis of narrative as more than a chronological sequence of events, and instead as endowed with "an order of meaning"; the narration of a sequence imposes a structure that imparts meaning to events.

The form/content dichotomy and subsequent emphasis on story structure guide the few studies of narrative constructions in network news. Smith (1988), for example, relies on Chatman's (1978) distinction between story (content) and discourse ("the means by which the content is communicated") in his analysis of narrative styles in network coverage of political party conventions. He uses this distinction to justify focusing on how (in what form) information was presented. Smith's (1988) analysis extends the application of narrative beyond identification of story type to the implications of story plot, but he stops short of transcending Chatman's approach to narrative structure as static.

Narrative is more than a structure. It is an *act*, the features of which

are functions of the variable sets of conditions in response to which they are performed. Accordingly, we might conceive of narrative discourse most minimally and most generally as verbal acts consisting of *someone telling someone else that something happened*. (Smith, 1981, p. 228)

The advantage of understanding narrative as act as well as structure is that it makes explicit the relation of narrative to interpretation. In other words, stories are meaningful not just because of their intrinsic structural relationships but also because of the degree to which audiences identify with the story.

For the news narrative, this relationship of form and function to the production of meaning implies that news stories need to be approached as selected representations of reality that structure events in symbolic narrative forms, and whose reception is determined by their appeal to the "fears, hopes, and prejudices of the cultures in which their audiences live" (Bennett & Edelman, 1985, p. 158). These tandem perspectives of form and function are sometimes mentioned in discussions of myth and drama; less often they are applied in a systematic way to extended televised news narratives. But news stories become meaningful through the composition of dramatic elements. Narratives "make news more interesting, even compelling, through dramatic representation; narrative forms, as Kenneth Burke observed, arouse and then satisfy expectations" (Cornfield, 1988, p. 182).

Several features of the news narrative contribute to the creation of drama. For a narrative to be credible, the narrator must command authority. The anchor accomplishes this by standing at the center of events, moving the story along "according to some larger pattern of meaning. . . . [S]he alone commands the whole body of problems, conflicts, and characters, and [s]he alone provides the continuous thread of meaning" (Sperry, 1981, p. 299). The tales the anchor narrates are built around themes of overt action that celebrate conquest over evil. When a problem arises, the protagonist and a few other supporting characters take some form of action to solve the problem. Sperry (1981, p. 301) explains this standard plot form:

> The world at peace is disrupted by some event (say, an act of terrorism). That event, which becomes the evil, is named and, if possible, analyzed and understood. It is then attacked by some leader, the hero figure, often a representative of the people. However, this leader, whether by choice or by the nature of his vocation, may not be able to meet the problem alone. So he gains allies, other leaders, and he also gains enemies—potential leaders who disagree with his plan of action, or rebels who align themselves with the evil. As these alignments become apparent, stories are then told of the effect of the problem on the average man. And, if the alignments become a matter more significant than the original event, we will also hear about the suffering of the average man as his appointed leaders fail to meet the problem.

The degree to which actual newscasts of terrorism follow this narrative structure has not been determined. But if news narratives follow this plot of an ineffective protagonist, they may frustrate audience expectations of resolution with a failed narrative of inaction. Additionally, journalistic exploitation of the dramatic elements in narrative plots of government incompetence in the face of terrorism and victimization of the average citizen may contribute to the escalation of terrorism as a public crisis.

NEWS AND THE CREATION OF CRISIS

The drama of a news story is obviously at its most intense during moments of crisis, and at times the threat of terrorism is presented as such a crisis. The role of the media in crisis situations is accentuated; the public has a heightened need for information, and thus the media's influence in defining reality increases (Howitt, 1982). But the determination of crisis status may be somewhat arbitrary. Altheide (1987) argues that the format of news creates crises from complex, historically located, and ongoing conflicts. He does not deny that "events of a crisis proportion do occur, but rather that mass-mediated perspective and the use of criteria to identify crises are quite distinctive" (p. 13). These criteria include: an ability to show the event easily and dramatically, a contrast with the status quo that appears to have consequences for a large number of people, the opportunity to show immediate victims who are interviewed expressing grief or sorrow, the ability to attribute blame, and the availability of a metaphorical term or phrase "graphically presented to give symbolic meaning to the whole issue" (Altheide, 1987). Arguably, these conditions exist in the telling of many news stories.

With the application of these criteria, then, almost any terrorist event can be presented as a crisis. Most studies of media coverage of terrorism that explore the implications of crisis designations by the media look at the Iranian hostage crisis at the end of Carter's presidency and criticize the media for overplaying the story (see, for example, Altheide, 1981, 1982; Diamond, 1982). Nimmo and Combs (1985) include a chapter on the Iranian hostage crisis in their book, *Nightly Horrors: Crisis Coverage by Television Network News.* Their focus is not on patterns of coverage of terrorism but on patterns of each network in reporting about crises in general. Thus, the implications of the crisis designation in network coverage of terrorism remain to be explored.

Given the remote and isolated nature of most terrorist acts, terrorism can be treated as a specific type of crisis, distinct from a catastrophe (the final event in or culmination of a development) or disaster (which implies great magnitude of loss in lives or property). Further, terrorism may be a "semantically created crisis," or one that engenders "widespread anxiety about an alleged threat that may or may not be real" (Edelman, 1977, p. 47). Edelman (1988) explains: "A crisis, like all news developments, is a creation of the language used to depict it; the appearance of a crisis is a political act, not a recognition of a fact or a rare situation" (p. 31). The implications of the semantically created crisis are considerable, for the crisis designation can become a tool to mobilize political support and justification for public sacrifices in the form of repressive policies. Television coverage of terrorism may contribute to the creation of the semantic crisis.

THE MEDIA ROLE IN DEFINING TERRORISM

The significance of terrorism as a form of political violence goes beyond its ability to instill fear and terror. Terrorism has also become a label commonly affixed to our most prominent foreign political adversaries, a label that has "acquired an extraordinary status in American public discourse," displacing communism as "public enemy number one" (Said, 1988, p. 149). This displacement is dramatic, for although there are groups that would call themselves communist, no group since 1940 has chosen to label itself as a terrorist one. The label of terrorist is given to a group rather than self-proclaimed, and the legitimacy of the label depends on the degree to which consensus is produced for that particular definition of political reality.

The analysis offered here attempts to demonstrate the centrality of news media in producing consensus about a dominant definition of terrorism. In defining deviance, news media turn to institutional sources, thus legitimizing definitions of public problems. As Hall et al. (1978) explain: "The structured relationship between the media and the primary institutional definers is that it permits the institutional definers to establish the initial definition or *primary interpretation* of the topic in question" (p. 58). The primary definition sets limits of discussion by framing the problem and conferring political responsibility for solving the problem. Gusfield (1981) calls this the "ownership of public problems," whereby a group with power, influence, and authority defines the public reality of a problem. Dominant definitions of reality are "owned" by the groups that reproduce them. The implications for ownership of such definitions of political violence and deviance are explored here with the problem of terrorism.

Although my focus is on media representations, the relationship of the media to the political institutions that define terrorism must be included to provide an understanding of how ownership is conferred and controlled. Hall (1982) explains: "For a meaning to be regularly reproduced, it [has] to win a kind of credibility, legitimacy, or taken-for-grantedness for itself. That involve[s] marginalizing, downgrading, or de-legitimating alternative constructions" (p. 67). The institutional definition of terrorism that replaced other definitions and gained credibility during the Reagan administration comes from the Department of State. For example, an Army journal notes a 1983 description of international terrorism subsequently abandoned by the State Department:

[T]he calculated use of violence or the threat of violence to attain goals political, religious, or ideological in nature . . . done through intimidation, coercion, and involving fear . . . (and) involves a criminal act that is often symbolic in nature and intended to influence an audience beyond the immediate victims. (Vought & Fraser, 1986, p. 74)

This definition contained the requisite of instilling fear through criminal violence, and it did not judge the motives of the actor. As in many definitions, the role of the state is ambiguous. By 1984, the Department of State provided a more restrictive and thus revealing definition that called terrorism "premeditated, politically motivated violence perpetrated against noncombatant targets by subnational groups or clandestine state agents" (Vought & Fraser, 1986, p. 73). This definition could have easily included guerrilla warfare and CIA campaigns; for the Department of State, the important shift was probably the emphasis on state-sponsored terrorism and consonance with the emerging "Shultz doctrine," which advocated military responses to terrorism and attempted to associate the Soviet Union with terrorism.

During Reagan's second term, definitions from the Department of State increasingly equated terrorism with specific groups the administration classified as enemies. For example, Paul Bremmer (1987), ambassador at large for counter-terrorism, provided this description: "Terrorism's most significant characteristic is that it despises and seeks to destroy the fundamentals of Western democracy—respect for individual life and the rule of law" (p. 1). And John Whitehead (1987, p. 70), deputy secretary of state, provided a similarly pointed definition:

What once may have seemed the random, senseless acts of a few crazed individuals has come into clearer focus as a new pattern of low-technology and inexpensive warfare against the West and its friends. . . . [T]errorism is a strategy and a tool of those who reject the norms and values of civilized people everywhere.

These anti-West slants pervaded the Reagan administration definitions. Media coverage of terrorism may have helped to equate terrorism with the enemies so labeled by the administration.

Shifting definitions also contributed to the creation of consensus about the magnitude of the terrorist threat by influencing statistics on the increase of terrorism. We tend to look at facts, particularly those grounded in statistics, as the most reliable and objective form of information. When facts are used to demonstrate the severity of a crisis or threat, they become dramatic. Statistics also serve an ideological function by grounding "free floating and controversial impressions in the hard, incontrovertible soil of numbers" (Hall et al., 1978, p. 9). In looking at statistics from a sociological perspective, Gusfield (1981) traced the "social history of a dramatic fact" to show the spurious origins of a "fact" that was used to dramatize and magnify the public problem of alcoholism. Broadcast news media reports of terrorism also include statistics from primary institutional definers that dramatize and exaggerate the frequency of terrorist activity. While "counter-definers" found no substantial increase in terrorism since 1980, administration officials reported dramatic increases, especially in acts against the United States. For instance, Bremmer (1987), writing in the *Department of State Bulletin*, cited 500 terrorist incidents occurring in 1983, 600 in 1984, and nearly 800 in 1985. Further, he reported that terrorism in 1986 caused 2,000 casualties (1987, p. 3). In contrast, Simon (1987), writing in *Foreign Policy*, stated that terrorist incidents aimed at U.S. targets peaked in 1977 with 99; in 1984, the U.S. share was 78, the lowest number in the past decade. The yearly average of international terrorist acts between 1980 and 1986 was 386 incidents. In 1985, "when more than 850 people were killed in international terrorist incidents, only 27 of the victims were Americans. And in 1986, the U.S. share of the 400 deaths was less than 3 per cent, or 11 people" (p. 108).

The discrepancy in statistics often depends on the definition used to classify data, and the criteria for labeling an act terrorist are neither clear nor consistent. The media's role in privileging particular statistics and creating dramatic facts is evident from the beginning of the Reagan administration. For instance, on March 11, 1981, ABC *World News Tonight* featured a CIA report that documented a "jump in worldwide assassinations" and a doubling of terrorist incidents from 1978 to 1980. However, assassinations do not necessarily constitute terrorist acts, for they have a specific target and goal that may not extend beyond the elimination of a single person. The creation of fear is not a primary objective of political assassination. Additionally, in 1980 the CIA revised its figures to include both a broader range of data sources and statistics on threats and hoaxes, which led to a "dramatic upward revision of figures" on terrorism (Wilkinson, 1986).

Stohl (1988) also referred to the CIA report in his discussion of the Reagan administration's "bureaucratic battle to redefine terrorism" and included Tom Wicker's comments on publication of the report:

The magic result . . . would be to double—from 3336 to 7000—the previously reported "incidents" of world terrorism from 1968 through 1979. The number killed or murdered, of course, would remain the same—about 800—since this bookkeeping sleight-of-hand merely makes the same situation look twice as bad as it did before. (p. 592)

This shift in statistical inventory was not mentioned in ABC's nightly newscast.

Selective perception and decontextualization often affect the accuracy of data on terrorist incidents (Laqueur, 1987). Although previous studies have explored the reproduction of definitions in the media, none has looked at the process by which definitions become official discourse, or the implications of this process in the creation of public knowledge. Media representation of statistics on the threat of terrorism constitutes a site whereby institutional definitions are legitimated and provides a point at which the relationship between news media and official discourse can be assessed.

AUDIENCE INTERPRETATIONS OF DRAMATIC NARRATIVES

Characteristics of the terrorist act itself also provide resources from which representations of terrorism are formed. Given the rhetorical strategy of terrorism as identified earlier, an approach to media coverage as drama is particularly appropriate. Gusfield (1981) explains that "conceptualizing public actions as drama means that we think about them *as if* they were performances artistically designed to create and maintain the attention and interest of an audience" (p. 175). It is easy to conceptualize media coverage of terrorism as a public action because both the news media and terrorists have audience-directed goals. Further, the violent nature of terrorism increases drama and therefore news value, making terrorist acts stand out against the routinized news treatment of crime and politically motivated violence.

Although terrorism is portrayed as more dramatic than other crimes, attention must be given to the way in which the criminal nature of the act helps determine the manner in which the act will be reported and subsequently interpreted by the audience. Knight and Dean (1982, p. 45) write that the

morally cohesive function of crime news points to the way in which news accounts, as a major form of constructing and transmitting social knowledge, are fundamentally ideological. . . . As bad news enters our heads openly through the front door, so order and normality reenter largely unnoticed through the back. . . . In this respect, the news media draw upon raw materials that are already fashioned in the wider ideology.

Coverage of terrorism may serve this morally cohesive function by helping legitimize administration labels of designated actors as terrorist villains. The wider ideology from which the media draw includes the attribution of Western rationality to terrorists and the removal of terrorist acts from social context. The approach to media coverage as a public drama of political violence helps locate media representations and audience responses to them within this wider ideological framework.

Analysis of the emergent news text of terrorism also illuminates the relationship between narrative form and function. At one level, "the consideration of the narrative qualities of news enables us to look more critically at whose values are encoded in news—whose stories are being told" (Bird & Dardenne, 1988, p. 79). At another level, analysis can assess the political implications of narratives that personify danger and substitute individuals for larger structural issues and conflicts.

CONCLUSION

Public perceptions of terrorism as an unprecedented threat to the maintenance of an orderly society have led to widespread anxiety, increasing pressure for government response, and more frequent calls for military strikes against political adversaries. Said (1988) has warned that the "wall-to-wall nonsense about terrorism can inflict grave damage . . . because it consolidates the immense, unrestrained pseudopatriotic narcissism we are nourishing" (p. 158). This "pseudopatriotic narcissism" shows the characteristics and potential consequences of a moral panic.

Moral panics arise when public anxiety connects with a dominant definition of deviance, and the anxiety is mobilized. Discussions of moral panics began with analysis of crime waves. Hall et al. (1978, p. 16) explain:

When the official reaction to a person, groups of persons or series of events is out of all proportion to the actual threat offered, when "experts," in the form of police chiefs, the judiciary, politicians and editors perceive the threat in all but identical terms, and appear to talk "with one voice" of rates, diagnoses, prognoses and solutions, when the media representations universally stress "sudden and dramatic" increases (in numbers involved or events) and "novelty," above and beyond that which a sober, realistic appraisal could sustain, then we believe it is appropriate to speak of the beginnings of a moral panic.

The emerging public perceptions of the threat posed by terrorism fit this description of moral panic. As has been noted, the actual incidents of terrorism worldwide have not increased dramatically, but international terrorism has been elevated to the status of national security threat. Reagan, former Secretary of Defense Caspar Weinberger, and former Secretary of State George Shultz have all come close to defining terrorist acts as acts of war. In 1985, Shultz said the United States was "pretty darn close to declaring war on Libya" (Simon, 1987). These proclamations and public acceptance of them effectively close debate about the viability of military retaliation, and the public more readily accepts repressive measures to combat terrorism. Additionally, as official reactions to the threat confer stature on it and create public frustration with government inaction, public pressure to retaliate against terrorists mounts. The U.S. bombing of Libya exemplified fulfillment of the public expectations that were cultivated by the cycle of depiction of terrorists, official reactions, and resulting public panic (Dobkin, 1989).

The panic reaction to terrorism is also symptomatic of a larger crisis in the international state system, in which the legitimacy of political actors and the boundaries of national sovereignty are continually shifting. Der Derian calls counterterrorism "an attempt to engender a new disciplinary order which can save the legitimacy principle of international relations. On a representational level, the spectacle of terrorism simultaneously displaces and distracts us from international disorder" (Der Derian, 1989, p. 234). Panic reactions have distracted attention from the causes of political violence and have unified public support for reactionary policies that have had "no positive impact on the deterrence, prevention and suppression of international terrorism." Neither have they "created a greater degree of safety for Americans traveling and living abroad" (Celmer, 1987, p. 113). Official reactions to terrorism may thus indicate a deeper distress over international disorder and an inability to formulate consistent policies to deal with it.

Additionally, the desire to exert military force in international affairs may contribute to the creation of the terrorist threat. As public hysteria over terrorism mounts, so does support for direct military action in foreign conflicts. This raises the level of acceptable violence as retaliation and permits presidents greater flexibility in determining the appropriateness of responses. A paradox arises, though, as action against terrorists escalates, for escalation serves the ends of the terrorist as well as the government actors who base foreign policy on military force. Although the motivations of public officials might not be uncovered here, this analysis does identify the process by which hysteria is created, or by which a problem is elevated to the status of crisis through media coverage of political violence.

4

What's in a Name? "Terrorism" as Ideograph

The statement, "one man's freedom fighter is another man's terrorist," has become a cliché that emerges frequently in discussions about definitions of terrorism. This cliché is commonly used to dismiss the relevance of definitional delineations with the caveat that any definition will have limitations and biases. But a common understanding of the term terrorism has emerged in public discourse, and the dismissal of definitional questions with culturally accepted truisms, such as the one above, diverts attention from the more problematic task of questioning the assumptions on which that understanding of terrorism is based.

Analysis of terms as ideographs provides one way to explore the creation and implications of words and symbols that provide a consensual, political orientation toward people or events. The idea that words embody action, or socially shared meanings with implications for behavior, has become a common orientation toward signs and their roles in discourse. Ideographs, though, express more than common values; they embody a normative commitment toward the telling of events and our responses to them. For instance, our stories of U.S. history are often organized around the ideograph of liberty, and this orientation shapes the perceptions we have about the foundations of democratic action. The signs of political culture that come to serve as ideographs thus command unique authority, and they provide a starting point for understanding the role of key terms in public discourse. Ideographs function in at least two ways in network news coverage of terrorism. As the building blocks in "vocabularies of political union and separation," ideographs define what is acceptable and what is to be condemned; they function "as guides, warrants, reasons, or excuses for behaviors and beliefs" (McGee, 1980, p. 6). Terrorism, as an aberrant behavior or set of actions, usually functions as a label of condemnation. Historically, however, it has not commanded the authority of an ideograph. Charting the evolution of the terrorist threat may reveal the function of television in elevating an emotive symbol to the level of ideograph. Further, by treating terrorism as an ideograph, we can understand how dominant representations of and assumptions about terrorism contribute to both our understanding of terrorism and the political force of that label. If, as Davis (1990) says, network news "serves to reify certain labels for persons, events, and situations" (p. 160), then ideographs are the culmination of that process of reification.

Ideographs may function not only within a fixed text but also as a conceptual orientation, or lens, through which events can be viewed. Hence the ideograph can serve as a journalistic frame through which terrorism is understood and representations of terrorist events are mediated. Frames are traditionally discussed as features of news selection and presentation. By following the development of ideographs in news coverage over time, we may see the emergence of a particular news frame for terrorism.

Ideographs do not stand in isolation; rather, they are built from a constellation of related terms. Additionally, ideographs such as terrorism may act in contraposition to other ideographs. During the cold war, "communism" stood as the epitome of evil, signifying a highly abstracted and ideological concept. "Communism" was contrasted with "democracy" as the representation of good. Both words, communism and democracy, signify highly abstracted and ideological concepts; each term opposes the other. Terrorism, however, operates at a lower level of abstraction. The term is relatively new to our common political lexicon, and it describes specific types of action rather than the collective beliefs, values, and behaviors of a nation. What, then, does the ideograph "terrorism" oppose? And does terrorism operate at the same level of abstraction as its antithetical ideograph?

During television newscasts from 1981 to 1986, "America" emerges as the antithesis of terrorism. Americans are treated as both the actual and symbolic targets of terrorism; terrorism exists primarily to fight America and all for which it stands—one nation, under God, with liberty and justice for all. Not surprisingly, then, these concepts—Judeo-Christian religion, freedom, and justice—form the basis of the cluster of terms that surround "American." And as this ideograph is extended in news coverage, terrorism concurrently becomes increasingly abstracted and generic. The movement of terrorism from an act of political violence to an ideograph is shown here through the characterizations of terrorism in television news. Characterizations "provide the first step in the move from the material experience of daily life to collective valuation through the simple process of providing concrete but motivationally loaded names to politically salient entities" (Lucaites & Condit, 1990, p. 7), and are thus the basis on which ideographs are built.

TERRORISM

As an umbrella term, terrorism encompasses many kinds of violent acts, including hijacking, bombing, kidnapping, occupation of buildings, sniping, arson, sabotage, theft, and suicide attacks. What distinguishes terrorism from these subsidiary terms is that terrorism imparts a political motive to the violent act and defines the target of the act as non-political, innocent, and outside of the political process the terrorist wishes to influence. A terrorist hijacking is a particular kind of hijacking; it is an attempt to attain political goals through fear or intimidation. Any definition of terrorism places emphasis on the political goal and thus distinguishes terrorism from other types of criminal activity.

Although definitions of terrorism emphasize political motivation to distinguish it from other criminal acts, characterizations of terrorism in the media typically emphasize terror. The term "terrorism" serves as a label of condemnation; the criminal act defined as a terrorist one suggests a deeper, uglier level of evil due to the sacrificial nature of the victim and the nefarious intent of the terrorist to traumatize. Terrorism plays on our most basic fears of the unknown and of dying; calling an act a terrorist one heightens our apprehension and fear of the perpetrator. It does not further our understanding of the causes of the act or the motivation of the actors.

Terrorism as Phenomenon

Early during the Reagan administration, ABC News established terrorism as a powerful evil that threatened the United States. Terrorism as a *label* was used sparingly. The emphasis was primarily on the tactics used by actors rather than the centrality of counterterrorism as a focal point for U.S. foreign policy. ABC News worked hard at establishing a generic context for terrorism. For example, during coverage of the March 2, 1981, hijacking of a Pakistan International Airlines B-720 by supporters of former Pakistani Prime Minister Zulfikar Ali Bhutto, the term "terrorist" was not used until March 10, eight days into the incident. From the first day of coverage, the hijackers' demands for the release of political prisoners were known; by March 6, we were informed that the "three men holding the plane" had already "shot and killed one of the passengers" after an established deadline had passed. Thus, the requisite conditions for the term "terrorist" to be applied to the hijackers existed long before the term surfaced in newscasts.

When the term was finally used on March 10, it brought with it no new information about the political motivation of the actors. It did, however, provide ABC News with an opportunity to launch a special assignment series on terrorism the next day. Anchor Peter Jennings introduced the series by saying: "Well, one thing we do know about the hijackers, they want the prisoners released, but like so many terrorists before them, they also want attention focused on their cause" (March 11, 1981). Attention to cause is not the kind of attention ABC News gave terrorists; rather, the Pakistani hijackers became part of a new "wave of terrorism" described in correspondent John McWethy's special assignment series. McWethy claimed that "the face of international terrorism is changing. Groups from nations all over the world are more sophisticated in picking their targets, and in the last twelve months, they're also more deadly." Brief attention to the motives of various terrorists was given; instead, McWethy focused on varieties of terrorism. "There's the right-wing Omega Seven" who are determined to "kill off Fidel Castro's regime" and the "Japanese Red Army, that seeks to destroy all governments, all forms of authority" (March 11, 1981). ABC News provided no information about the Pakistani incident, the incident that gave rise to the series on terrorism, beyond calling the tactic passé: "Despite this week's hijacking to Damascus, experts believe this tactic has all but passed from the terrorist handbook for the 1980s" (March 11, 1981).

The absence of background information continued throughout coverage of the hijacking. The next day, Jennings announced: "Whoever [the hijackers] turn out to be, their names will be recorded on a long list of men and women who wish to change the world—or at least their part of it" (March 12, 1981). ABC News did not discuss why or in what ways these people wished to change the world, thus rendering these topics irrelevant; terrorists were described only by the nature of their actions. They formed "underground political death squads from all over the world" who were determined to "wage war on modern society. . . . Virtually thousands of young men and women learn how to murder and destroy for their causes." These "groups of killers" were supported by Cuba, the Soviet Union, and Libya. Terrorists posed a "chilling threat to the civilized world," and some were "little more than pathological killers" (March 13, 1981). The issue of why a Pakistani airplane was hijacked was answered by identifying who performed the act, and as long as the "who" was a terrorist, the action was explained through characterizations of terrorism.

Later in 1981, when Brigadier General James Dozier was kidnapped in Italy by the Red Brigades, ABC News used the terrorism label in the first full day of coverage. It was once again part of the wider phenomenon of "Italian terrorism." ABC News told viewers that Dozier was kidnapped because he was a NATO officer and an American. Although this was the first Red Brigades operation against a military officer and a foreigner, ABC News warned us that "this kidnapping both recaptures the headlines and raises the campaign to an international level" (Dec. 18, 1981). The motives of the Red Brigades were reduced to colorful phrases taken from their five lengthy communiqués. ABC News reported that Dozier would be "tried in people's court" because he was "a NATO hangman" (Dec. 18, 1981) and "an assassin hero of American massacres in Vietnam" (Dec. 27, 1981), and that one faction within the Red Brigades had threatened to kill another Red Brigades group (Jan. 3, 1982). Between Dozier's capture on December 17 and his rescue over a month later on January 28, there were no background reports on the Red Brigades as a political group or on the relationship of Italian politics to terrorism. The only contextual information about the Red Brigades provided by ABC's coverage appeared in the form of two references to similarities between the Dozier kidnapping and the Red Brigades' abduction and murder of former Italian Prime Minister Aldo Morro (Dec. 27, 1981; Jan. 7, 1982).

Of course, providing context for terrorist events might have left networks open to charges of complicity or sympathy. Davis (1990) explains that an attempt to supply this kind of information "poses risks that are generally unacceptable.

Selection of background information typically can imply a perspective and can easily be seen to bias a story" (p. 169). Networks attempt to minimize this risk by using special assignment reports or commentaries, but these reports provide background on the threat of terrorism as an epidemic rather than on specific terrorist groups or their motivations. For instance, during the Pakistani hijacking, nearly half of all ABC News coverage dealing with the incident was devoted to the special assignment series on terrorism.[1] All three parts of the series concentrated on the threat of terrorism, starting with reminders of the Iran hostage crisis, which, according to ABC News, proved to us that a "superpower" could be "immobilized by the terrorists" (March 11, 1981), and continuing with glimpses of the atrocities performed by "the more than 100 terrorist groups operating in the world" and aimed at the United States, a "target of major opportunity" (March 12, 1981). Finally, ABC News provided scenarios of how terrorists might strike "at home," because our country is a "sitting duck" (March 13, 1981). Unfortunately, rather than risk appearing complicitous, television news abandons explanation, filling the contextual void with special reports that bolster the privileged status of terrorism as a threat to national security.

Reports such as these provided the only conceptual schema for terrorist events and told about the danger of an incomprehensible evil, thus legitimizing a decontextualized, generic frame by which terrorist acts were interpreted. Laqueur (1987, p. 9) explains the liabilities of this generic approach to terrorism:

[T]here is no terrorism *per se*, except perhaps on an abstract level, but different terrorisms. It does not follow that there is no room for objective statements on the subject, that we cannot pass judgment, and should not take action. But each situation has to be viewed in its specific, concrete context, because terrorism is dangerous ground for *simplificateurs* and *generalisateurs*.

The different terrorisms were obscured in network newscasts, and terrorism became the more compelling "scourge" of evil.

The Terrorist as Archetypal Enemy

The tendency to group terrorists together according to decontextualized acts of violence not only obscures differences but also facilitates the creation of the archetypal terrorist. Although early descriptions of terrorists remained vague, the bombing of the Marine barracks in Beirut and subsequent, highly publicized terrorist acts in the Middle East provided models for composition of the archetypal enemy: the Islamic terrorist. Between 1980–85 there were more than four times as many anti-American terrorist incidents in Latin America than in the Middle East (Laqueur, 1987); nonetheless, Islam came to represent terrorism in ABC News broadcasts.

Against the backdrop of the Iran hostage crisis, such characterizations might not seem surprising. As Said (1981) wrote: "It was the leap from a specific experience—unpleasant, anguished, miserably long in duration—to huge generalizations about Iran and Islam that the hostage return licensed in the media and in the culture at large" (p. xxiii). When, beginning in the fall of 1983 and culminating in 1985, Middle East tensions provoked terrorist acts involving Americans, journalists fully exploited this license through their characterizations of terrorism, reifying and refining the ideograph.

The most dramatic act of terrorism that returned media attention to the Middle East following the Iran hostage crisis was the bombing of the U.S. Marine and French military barracks in Beirut. Although other terrorist acts, such as the May 1982 bombing of the French Embassy in Beirut, commanded media attention, none rivaled the degree of coverage given to the attack on the Marine barracks. During the two evening newscasts before the U.S. invasion of Grenada (Oct. 23 and 24, 1983), ABC News spent 18:00 and 19:20 minutes respectively (out of nearly 22 minutes) on coverage of the bombings. The term "terrorist" was used sparingly in the newscasts; on October 23, 1983, the day of the bombing, the act was described as a terrorist one only twice, and there were only three references to terrorists "linked to Iran's Khomeini regime" (Oct. 23, 1983).

ABC News did not give a possible motivation for the act on the first day of coverage, and the ascription of the terrorist label to crisis events was not yet a standard feature of television news. One probable reason for using caution with the label might have been due to the comment such a designation made about U.S. policy in Lebanon. ABC News devoted considerable time to discussions of "one more casualty—domestic support for the president's policy" (Oct. 23, 1983). ABC News aired statements by then Secretary of Defense Weinberger, who mentioned the difficulty of the mission and the possibility of a temporary withdrawal of the Marines to off-coast ships; former Secretary of State Henry Kissinger, who emphasized the ineffectiveness of U.S. policy; and a series of comments made by congressional opponents of the U.S. military mission in Lebanon (Oct. 23, 1983):

> Former U.S. Representative Samuel Stratton (D-N.Y., 23rd): I think the Marines ought to be pulled out right away. I think it's perfectly clear that the mission that they had been assigned they are unable to carry out.
>
> Sen. Ernest Hollings (D-S.C.): It's a totally inadequate kind of assignment for 1,200 Marines, hunkered down at the end of a runway and told to sit still and be killed.
>
> Sen. Sam Nunn (D-Ga.): No, I do not think this administration has ever defined the mission in a logical way, at least the military mission.
>
> Sen. Charles Mathias (R-Md.): We have known what the mission was, it was to be a presence, it was a symbolic presence. But I think that [in] the events of the last twelve hours that mission has evaporated.

Of course, these statements were balanced with those from members of Congress "who backed the compromise to keep the Marines in Lebanon," but the report closed with information that "Senate Majority Leader Baker" had "immediately urged the president in a private letter to get the Marines out" (Oct. 23, 1983). If the purpose of the bombing was to force a reevaluation of U.S. policy in the Middle East and eventual withdrawal of the Marines, then the terrorist act was a success. But this objective was never identified as the motive behind the suicide attack, perhaps precisely because the act achieved its intended effect.

Alternative explanations of motive were offered on the second day of coverage. Peter Jennings introduced a report on the main suspects in the bombing this way:

Well, we don't know with certainty who planned or carried out the attack. Yesterday, a group called the Free Islamic Revolution movement said it was responsible; today, another group, the Islamic Holy War, claims the credit. *One point about the Middle East—sometimes what people believe is more important than what they can prove. People act on their beliefs.* Shortly after the attack on the Marines and the French, the finger pointing began. (Oct. 24, 1983; emphasis added)

Jennings's comment about the importance of beliefs over evidence supported the characterization of Iranians as irrational, as he implied that people in the Middle East are motivated and convinced by unsubstantiated beliefs rather than evidence.

Similarly, ABC correspondent Mike Lee told viewers that "these revolutionary guards of Ayatollah Khomeini," presumably the two groups to which Jennings referred, "are widely believed to have trained and supplied an extremist Lebanese Shi'ite group known as Jihad." Lee listed several terrorist acts thought to have been carried out by Jihad, and continued:

Based on the available evidence, the group which claimed responsibility for the Beirut bombing of U.S. Marines, the Free Islamic Revolutionary Movement, appears to be part of that same Lebanese Shi'ite fringe allied with those Iranian commandoes based in Lebanon's Bekaa Valley. . . . As to the motive? Iran has threatened to retaliate against the French for furnishing [arms] to Iraq in the Gulf War. The Ayatollah Khomeini has threatened to strike out against the United States for America's plans to keep the Strait of Hormuz open. (Oct. 23, 1983)

Lee's reference to "*that* same Lebanese Shi'ite fringe" and "*those* Iranian commandoes" imparted equivalency to all of the groups, defining them solely as agents of Khomeini, or, as the interpretation was later extended, as "pro-Iranian Lebanese extremists" or "pro-Iranian Lebanese fanatics" who were "manipulated" by Syrian President Hafez el-Assad "into carrying out the final stages of the operation."

Moreover, the motives attributed to the acts were specific, discrete, and unrelated to the presence of U.S. Marines and French troops in Lebanon. These attributions blurred distinctions in a manner typical within the ideograph of terrorism, and they dismissed the agenda explicitly claimed by the Islamic Holy War at the time of the bombing: "Violence will remain our only path if they [foreign forces] do not leave. We are ready to turn Lebanon into another Vietnam. We are not Iranians, or Syrians, or Palestinians. We are Lebanese Moslems" (Mickolus et al., 1989, p. 451). Although ABC News reported that a call was made, details of the call were not given. The ideograph did not allow distinctions among Islamic terrorists or explicit recognition of the effectiveness of the attack.

With their coverage of the attacks on the French and American barracks in 1983, ABC reinforced popular perceptions of Islamic terrorism. In subsequent newscasts, they further caricatured and depoliticized terrorists, and, more generally, Arabs. These characterizations served as an orientation for interpreting events. As Carey (1986) writes, "When the description becomes fine-grained enough, how merges into why: a description becomes an explanation" (p. 149). Since our understanding of terrorism evolved through characterizations of the archetypal terrorist, these depictions deserve closer scrutiny.

ABC's terrorists of the 1980s possessed several unifying features. These terrorists were produced by cultures that breed terrorism, they were outcast and destitute, and they were suidical, religious fanatics. The influence of culture in cultivating terrorism was clearest in descriptions of Lebanon. Beginning in June 1985, ABC attributed a recent "rash of hijackings" to "anarchy in Lebanon," where "most of the terrorists have come from" (June 14, 1985). Beirut was described as "one of the most violent places on earth" (June 22, 1985), and Jennings portrayed the Lebanese people as violent:

We sometimes think everyone in Lebanon carries a gun. That isn't true. But there are probably more guns per capita than there are almost anywhere in the world. Many Shi'ite children do grow up with grievances, and very often with guns. (June 25, 1985)

Jennings was trapped by his own stereotype; he identified and attempted to counter the militaristic image of the Lebanese, but then provided a depiction that supported that very image. The malaise of Lebanon, with its lawlessness, its "shifting mosaic of factions" (June 25, 1985) and "shadowy, faceless ranks of terrorists" (June 18, 1985), reached as far as the Shi'ite community of Dearborn, Michigan, where "the immigrants" have "escaped the ravages of the homeland, only to find Mideast tensions have a long reach" (June 19, 1985). Although all Shi'ites might not have been terrorists, their Lebanese affiliation condemned them to "pain and suffering" because of the Lebanese propensity for irrational violence.

According to ABC News, "Shi'ite Muslims" were also outcast and destitute, "the losers in life":

The people who've been pushed from their homes in the south. The refugees who are crammed into deserted buildings and shanty towns that straddle the edge of Beirut. They've always been the underdog, and they've always been the community that was taken for granted in Lebanon. That is why Amal was created, originally a movement whose main goal was to improve living conditions. Amal has become the force to be reckoned with in this country. (June 21, 1985)

Once again, explanation lay buried in description. Shi'ites were not just underdogs; they were underclass Lebanese living "out in the tumble-down, teeming Shi'ite tenements" (June 17, 1985), the "Beirut Shi'ite slums" (June 27, 1985). The descriptions were vivid; after all, we usually reserve adjectives such as "teeming" for rats or cockroaches.

Condemnation of Islam also took subtler forms in the newscasts. For example, Jennings editorialized with comments such as: "A warning today from Islamic Holy War, *whatever it is*" (July 2, 1985; emphasis added); "those Palestinian terrorists who insist on battling Israel to the bitter end are expressing their view in their customary way" (visuals show a coffin draped with an Israeli flag; Oct. 9, 1985); "the *so-called* Islamic Jihad has sent a message to news agencies in London" (Dec. 31, 1985; emphasis added); and "there is no way of knowing whether the letter was actually sent by anyone connected with Islamic Jihad, *whatever it is*" (Jan. 13, 1986; emphasis added). Each of these phrases signalled ridicule, an attitude that there would be no value in understanding the motivations or social context of an Islamic voice.

Jennings's dismissal of Islamic terrorists made sense within the context of the ideograph. Terrorists were not only "the losers in life," produced by lawless, violent cultures; they were also "ferocious, vicious," religious fanatics (July 1, 1985) who attempted to indoctrinate Americans as well as their own youth (June 24, 1985). The "religious fervor" of terrorists (June 26, 1985) made them both more powerful and more evil, and their influence reached beyond individual acts of violence. Terrorist incidents that required several days of coverage gave ABC the opportunity to develop these characterizations. For instance, during the 1985 hijacking of TWA Flight 847, ABC used a report on the indoctrination of Amal terrorists to fill the gap in, as Jennings put it, "how little we know about people like those in Amal and their grievances" (June 25, 1985). Betsy Aaron gave this background on Amal:

> Aaron (in voice over): Indoctrination begins early. He is only four, and "Amal" is one of his first spoken words. Boys are trained to do men's work, and they do it with a casualness because it is the only life most have ever known. Anyone can join Amal. And most Shi'ite males do. Basic training lasts 15 days; then you are a fighter. To rise in the ranks, there is more training. And more indoctrination.
>
> Amal instructor, through translator: We are going to destroy the Israeli forces. And if you get killed, you will be a martyr. Victory, or martyrdom.
>
> Aaron (on camera, closing report): There are few, if any, subtleties in a fighter's life. In Baobek, the prayer for martyrdom is as strong as the prayer for victory. Militia duty is not a school or a job; it is a life. And it is never too early for a Shi'ite to begin. (June 25, 1985)

The emphasis in Aaron's report was on fanaticism, on the willingness of terrorists to die, and on their prayers for martyrdom.

Although such depictions centered on Lebanese Shi'ites, ABC extended these portrayals to terrorism in general. Jennings began one report: "Another example today of the kind of terrifying fanaticism which exists in Lebanon. The Shi'ite Amal militia in Southern Lebanon is showing this film to school children." The film showed an aerial view of a car pulling out on an empty street and moving toward a military convoy; the car exploded while approaching the other vehicles. The children "are shown a picture of the driver of the car. He died in that blast. A martyr, the children are told, to their cause. Terrorists who hijack planes and take hostages are fanatics, too" (July 4, 1985). This segment was aired on July 4, Independence Day; U.S. hostages in Beirut had been released five days earlier, so the piece was not relevant primarily for the information it provided about an unfolding event, but for the contrast it gave between American notions of freedom and Islamic tools of indoctrination. ABC's report also reified the media's belief in "some deep connection between suicide and the Shi'ite faith," a link that, as Laqueur (1987, p. 231) has noted, "was grossly exaggerated":

In the attacks of Al Jihad al Islam (the most militant of the terrorist sects) only five or six were carried out by people bent on committing suicide (three or four in Beirut, one or two in Kuwait). . . . [O]f the perpetrators, some were not Shi'ites, some were mentally disturbed, and the others were apparently under the influence of drugs. Since 1984 there have been no more suicide operations.

Although some forms of fanaticism may prompt an occasional suicide attack, there is no necessary relationship between the two. For instance, "more Irish Catholic terrorists have thus far committed suicide than Shi'ites, although Catholic belief unequivocally opposes suicide" (Laqueur, 1987, p. 231).

Nonetheless, ABC's penchant for portrayals of suicidal, religious fanaticism as the trademark of Islamic terrorism continued throughout the 1980s. Palestinians were likely to strike "on the West Bank and anywhere else any Palestinian fanatic thinks he can make a public point, whether it's seajacking the *Achille Lauro* or murdering three Israelis on holiday in Cyprus" (Oct. 9, 1985), and viewers were warned that more attacks were "already planned by the so-called martyrs, bent on suicide as well as murder" (Dec. 12, 1985). The point is not that no terrorists are fanatics; most are probably deeply committed to their cause. More importantly, terrorists vary in their convictions, motivations, nationality, and political goals. Even among Islamic terrorists, religion is understood in a variety of ways, and a singular profile of the Middle Eastern terrorist is impossible to compile (Kramer, 1987). Finally, although the portrait of the Islamic religious fanatic as terrorist provides a face for an archetypal enemy, it obscures the reality of other forms of terrorism.

Distinctions

Ideographs are never seamless; one group can never exercise complete control over the meaning of a symbol. In support of textual openness, or the possibility of interpretations other than a dominant one, some critics argue for "less attention to the textual strategies of preference or closure and more to the gaps and spaces that open up meanings not preferred by the textual structure" (Fiske, 1987, p. 64). Gaps did exist in ABC's characterizations of the terrorist, but although references to distinctions between types of terrorists sometimes surface, these differences are always portrayed within the dominant frame. Jennings would comment:

The Shi'ites you saw there, they may be treating the hostages as well as the hostages say, but in another part of town they are still attacking Palestinians. Sieges of the Palestinian camps have been underway for many days now; there's been no let-up. And that is the two sides of the Amal we're dealing with. (June 20, 1985)

The "two sides of Amal" were the two sides of a personality rather than sides in a political struggle.

The most striking example of resistance to the dominant frame came in ABC's coverage of TWA Flight 847 hostage Allyn Conwell. In a taped interview with ABC reporters, Conwell pleaded the case of the Amal and attempted to distinguish them from the original hijackers of the plane:

I will make an appeal . . . based on the reading that we've done since getting here, and that has been considerable. We understand that the hostages, I call them hostages for valid reasons, the Lebanese people that are held in Israel, are held contrary to the Geneva Accord. So, yes, I say, Israel, please release those people, not because there are 39 hostages captured in Lebanon, but simply because it's the right thing to do. . . . [M]any in our group have a profound sympathy for their cause, for the reasons the Amal have in saying, Israel, free my people. . . . [Amal] are indeed capitalizing on the situation, but . . . if someone captured my wife and children and held them across that border, I also would be taking drastic actions and doing things that would be, indeed, against my principles to secure their freedom. (June 27, 1985)

Conwell's statements continually challenged the depiction of terrorists as insane and less than human, and he attempted to clarify distinctions between Amal factions. After his release, Conwell was asked to repudiate his statements. Jennings queried, "Mr. Conwell, you had a great many compliments . . . about the people who were holding you. Do you wish to say the same things today, now that you're a free man?" (July 1, 1985). Jennings allowed Conwell to repeat his distinctions between groups of Shi'ites before interrupting him and turning to the other former hostages.

The implication sustained by the network was that Conwell was under pressure, perhaps even brainwashed by the terrorists. Statements from other former hostages such as Peter Hill repudiated Conwell: "I'm so angry and frustrated that, personally, I'd like to get even. They're animals, absolute animals. *I wasn't taken in by the garbage they tried to indoctrinate us with*" (July 7, 1985; emphasis added). Conwell represented a challenge to popular depictions of Islamic terrorists, and his statements were promptly discredited.

Finally, in January 1986, three months before the U.S. launched a bombing raid against Libya, ABC News noted the problematic nature of accepting institutional definitions of terrorism. Jennings introduced the final report of a five-part series on terrorism: "Before the world can deal effectively with terrorism, there has to be wider agreement on what a terrorist is. . . . In other words, what we may see so clearly as terrorism, others may see as struggle." Barrie Dunsmore concluded the series:

It is precisely because one man's terrorist is another man's freedom fighter that international attempts to curb terrorism have substantially failed. Retaliation may provide some temporary satisfaction, but it usually results in an escalation of violence. History suggests that terrorism is ended when the political and social conditions which produce terrorists are somehow changed. (Jan. 17, 1986)

In three sentences, Dunsmore summarized key limitations of the ideograph of terrorism. But although the network did occasionally attempt to explain the perspective of dissenters, thus showing gaps in the ideograph, these points of resistance were eclipsed by ABC's constant reification of the dominant frame.

Close inspection of any stereotype will reveal its limitations and biases. Media coverage of terrorism, however, has created an ideograph that discourages this kind of inspection. Condit (1987) comments on the power of the ideograph to limit polysemic interpretation of texts: "It is precisely the ability of dominant groups to abstract words-as-empirical-units from their vocabularies (especially law) with tightly controlled meanings that gives dominant elites enhanced social power through the manipulation of popular language" (p. 48). The ideograph of terrorism provides the framework for interpreting all subsequent actions of a group so labeled. International terrorists are not all examples of Islamic, "suicidal, religious fanatics" (Jan. 13, 1986), or the archetypal terrorist presented in ABC News. However, creation and perpetuation of the archetype through depictions of the Islamic terrorist and elevation of terrorism to ideograph give force to the label and empower terrorists, not by our recognition of their grievances or political motivations, but by our increased fear of terrorists as irrational, fanatic criminals.

THE AMERICAN IDEOGRAPH

Without the development of a political context for or grievances of terrorism, these enemies could seem unfocused and without motivation. But as terrorist acts became more horrifying and the ideograph of terrorism grew increasingly terrifying, Americans were simultaneously celebrated, glorified, and eulogized. The destruction of Americans and their values came to serve as the unifying motivation of terrorists; just as Soviet leader Nikita Khrushchev said in the early 1960s that he would bury capitalist countries, terrorists in the 1980s were portrayed as determined to destroy the United States and its allies. As Marine Commandant P.X. Kelley said in the wake of the bombing of the Marine barracks, "There are skilled and professional terrorists out there right now who are examining our vulnerabilities and making devices which are designed to kill Americans" (Oct. 31, 1983).

Terrorists designed weapons to kill Americans because Americans represented the forces of good in the world. They were, according to ABC News, "symbols of American power, that is, a superpower that represents Western ideas, Western technology and economic power. The terrorists see it as a symbol they must attack" (June 26, 1985). Since, according to the ideograph, terrorists are irrational and embody evil, hatred of what is good suffices as a plausible motive for terrorist action.

As terrorism functions as a term of political separation, the ideograph of the United States allows unification. During the hijacking of TWA Flight 847, ABC News emphasized that the hostages were "ordinary people, . . . just some people who took a plane ride and now are in danger simply because of who they are: Americans. People with whom 237 million other Americans can identify and so feel all the more outraged" (June 17, 1985). Viewers identified with hostages and victims not just because of shared citizenship, but also because of shared values. TWA Captain Testrake's statement on his release provided the constellation of terms on which the ideograph is based:

To the people of America, we are proud and honored knowing how you joined together in our time of crisis to let it be known that our country was behind us 100 percent. It was your thoughts and prayers that gave us strength and kept our minds on our main goal: freedom. (July 2, 1985)

Americans derive pride from their morality, their freedom, and their self-determination; they are the antithesis of terrorists. In the context of terrorism, these ideographs do more than make the simple distinction between "us" and "them"; by portraying the ideographs as dialectically opposed, television news imparts equal levels of abstraction to the terms. McGee and Martin (1983) note the creation of false dilemmas with ideological arguments that reduce "complex material instances to binary categories of choice" (p. 59). Presenting terrorism as an ideological opposite to the United States empties terrorism of both political motivation and historic context.

A Nation under God

The power of terrorism as an ideograph depends in part on its relationship to antithesis. After all, for terrorism to command a crisis response, it must embody a direct threat to the values and beliefs of Americans. Several themes that characterize television coverage of terrorism provide this direct contrast to the ideograph of terrorism. First, unlike the religious fanaticism of Islam, Americans were portrayed as devout Christians (or, perhaps, Jews) whose support for hostages, victims, and their families came in the form of prayer. General Dozier's wife went to "a special Mass offered for his safe return" (Dec. 22, 1981); hostage families were continually praying (June 14, 1985; June 23, 1985; June 24, 1985; June 26, 1985; June 29, 1985; July 4, 1985); and the resolution of terrorist crises brought praise to God.

Allyn Conwell thanked God for the return of the TWA 847 hostages; an *Achille Lauro* passenger cried, "Praise the Lord, my sister and my husband are free" (Oct. 9, 1985). Americans were portrayed as believers, because "when you have your faith in God, that's all you need" (Oct. 11, 1985), and "it is through the power of prayer that so many of [the hostages] have been delivered safely" (former hostage William McDonnell, June 23, 1985).

In addition to frequent mention of prayer, ABC News highlighted the religious activities of Americans victimized by terrorism. Passengers on TWA 847 were "making a religious pilgrimage" when the plane was hijacked (June 14, 1985); one of their cockpit crew, Benjamin Zimmerman, was "called 'Christian' by his friends; he happens to be a minister. . . . He is deeply religious, and when he has time to himself he often flies into very remote areas to preach the gospel" (June 19, 1985). Robert Stethem, who was killed during the hijacking, was eulogized as a "born-again Christian" who "had a confidence in God that was unbendable" (July 5, 1985). Americans were shown to be pious people who stood in contrast to the dark and alien nature of Islamic fundamentalism.

The appeals that Americans made to terrorists for the release of hostages on religious grounds made sense given the framing of terrorists as religious fanatics. ABC News gave official legitimacy to this idea, and told viewers that the State Department "recognized religion as a natural means of contact between the two estranged cultures" during the Iranian hostage crises of 1979–80 (July 4, 1985). During coverage of Independence Day activities, ABC News broadcast statements appearing on Middle Eastern television stations that had been made by families of hostages still in captivity: "We're all God's children, and I beg you in his name to free Terry"; "Please, in the name of God that you and I share, end our torment"; "I appeal to you, in the name of God, to release my husband"; and "God bless you, and peace be with you, much love" (July 4, 1985). Although the families of hostages were understandably distraught and trying various means to obtain the release of the hostages, by airing these statements, ABC News supported its own attributions of simplistic motivations to terrorists and reflected a deep misunderstanding of the various branches of Islam.

Liberty and Justice

As champions of the "free world," Americans are proud of their liberty and the opportunity to exercise their will. ABC News focused on these attributes of American pride and showed Americans refusing to be intimidated by terrorists. For instance, although travel to Europe dropped by 20 percent after the December 1985 massacres at the Rome and Vienna airports, people interviewed by ABC News said they were "willing to play the odds" (Jan. 1, 1986). Three months later, following the bombing of TWA flight 840, Americans "said they were concerned about the attack, but intended to keep flying." As one woman said, "You can't let other people, you know, dictate what you're going to do" (April 2, 1986). Even the husband of a bombing victim affirmed this sense of determination: "Life's too short. You have to go where you want, do what you want, when you want" (April 6, 1986). The American values of freedom and self-determination became evident in the optimistic defiance of the people selected by ABC News.

With freedom came the expectation of justice, which took many forms; American ideology incorporates various versions of distributive, procedural, and retributive justice. In coverage of terrorism, justice most often began with procedural issues. ABC News presented the claims of several designated experts who defined justice in this manner. Terrorists "must be dealt justice" (Reagan, June 25, 1985) or "brought to justice" (Reagan, July 1, 1985; Testrake, July 3, 1985; Redman, Oct. 15, 1985); Americans want to see "justice done" (Reagan, Oct. 11, 1985; Klinghoffer, Oct. 28, 1985), and to "prosecute those sons of bitches" (Ambassador Valiotes, Oct. 10, 1985).

The magnitude of evil posed by terrorism required more than procedural justice, though; it called for retribution or revenge. ABC News showed Reagan as determined that the TWA 847 hijackers would "pay for what they did" (July 2, 1985). In the *Achille Lauro* incident, Reagan "sought out reporters to publicly demand that the hijackers be punished," and he confessed that he "was thinking, mad as I am, of vengeance instead of justice" (Oct. 10, 1985). American outrage legitimized this form of justice. As one citizen said, "I really don't care whether the PLO kills [the hijackers], whether Reagan kills them—I would kill them if I could" (Oct. 10, 1985). Since America is strong and just, the United States must exert its power and take revenge for terrorist action. That is the "right" thing to do. Thus, the ideograph of the United States provides basic values from which journalists can build stories revolving around the need to carry out retributive justice.

CONCLUSION

The polarity of Americans and terrorists as ideographs provides frames for guiding journalistic interpretation of terrorist acts. Terrorists have become part of the wider phenomenon of terrorism, defined by its tactics alone and without clear or rational political motivation. By taking the politics out of terrorism and concentrating on the horror inflicted by suicidal, Islamic, religious fanatics, ABC News magnified the incomprehensibility of terrorism. And the media's use of the ideograph of Americans as the actual and symbolic targets of terrorism has confined Middle Eastern conflicts to ones of "us" against "them" rather than exploring broader issues of geo-political struggles and the inherent instability of most developing countries.

Ideographs are building blocks of political discourse, and they provide frames by which journalists orient themselves toward an event, or categories into which events such as terrorist acts can be placed. Once these definitional frames have been learned, we continue to act on them without evaluating these frames and without understanding the process by which we came to accept them. They become institutionalized, part of the common-sense understanding of legislators and journalists. In this manner, the ideograph of terrorism has come to function as a semantic frame, for it defines terrorism regardless of the specific story into which the ideograph is placed. Semantic frames are a primary step in creating consensus and are the orientations on which structural frames, or narrative forms, are built.

NOTE

1. Of the 29 minutes and 50 seconds devoted to the hijacking of the Pakistani jet, 15 minutes and 30 seconds were spent on coverage of the incident, and 14 minutes, 20 seconds were spent on the special assignment series that accompanied the event coverage.

5

Paper Tigers and Video Postcards: Narrative Framing in Network News

Just as we have grand narratives by which we organize and give meaning to the events in our lives, journalists have organizing principles inherent in their profession. These journalistic principles, referred to earlier as frames, are a grounding construct in analysis of news narratives. Through frames, journalists determine what counts as news, how to define an event, and which facts are relevant to a story. Although terrorists and other political adversaries gain publicity from television news coverage, this publicity is mediated by the structural constraints of the news story.

Standard applications of news frames treat them as an angle or orientation by which a happening is defined as a news event. These "semantic" frames are formed from journalistic values and ideographs; they direct the journalist's apprehension of an event. Semantic frames can be distinguished from structural ones, which provide narrative forms. Structural frames are culturally embedded orders of meaning; that is, narratives transform events into a culturally salient structure that allows them to be disseminated, understood, and perpetuated. Events are thus experienced not as a collection of facts, but as a value-laden paradigm of behavior. Narratives and ideographs act together; semantic frames provide value orientations that are used and developed in, or created by, structural frames, or story forms.

Narratives thus provide the formal conventions by which acts are understood. The process of framing events according to specific narrative structure imparts value and motivation to those events; as White (1981) explains, "Story forms not only permit us to judge the moral significance of human projects, they also provide the means by which to judge them, even while we pretend to be merely describing them" (p. 253). This act of framing an event within the structure of narrative differs from semantic framing, or defining the initial perception of an event.

In network news coverage of international terrorism, structural frames evolve from and create background oppositions provided by ideographs such as "terrorism" and "America." These terms serve as a natural basis for story forms based on dramatic tension. Conflict and dramatic tension are central components in any narrative, as is the implication of resolution. In this sense, narrative form is predictable, and it sets up expectations on the part of audiences. A former CBS newscaster, Fred Graham, noted the reliance of television journalists on standard narrative structure: "News stories on CBS tended to become two-minute morality plays with heroes or villains and a tidy moral to be summoned up at the end." Despite the fact that "many important events did not present clear-cut heroes, villains, or morals," Graham said, "correspondents became experts at finding them" (in Yardley, 1990, p. 36). This imposed narrative structure of an emotional, ethical drama with clearly demarcated protagonists and villains is characteristic of melodrama. In it, "one resolution is possible; the victory of the forces of clear good over the forces of clear evil. Only one option is afforded to the (attending) audience; to applaud the hero and boo the villain" (Wagner-Pacifici, 1986, p. 279). Melodrama is thus treated here as more than a theatrical, sensational style of storytelling; it is also a plot structure that relies on moral action of protagonists rather than the development of characters or dimensions of conflict.

Television's reliance on melodramatic forms can be explained partly by economic motives. Other narrative structures abound in American culture; for instance, stories can be told as comedies, ironies, or tragedies as well as melodramas. But the latter form is comfortable and pleasing to television audiences, and program sponsors can be expected to welcome a format that reassures and satisfies audiences. Since they are organized around a quest or conquest of evil, melodramatic narratives unify audiences and provide communal goals. They celebrate the central virtues of a community and reinforce conceptions of authority through the ritualistic defeat of a perceived evil.

Melodrama thus mitigates moral ambiguity by presenting a bifurcated world, one that is well suited to the demands of contemporary television news reporting styles. In television news and entertainment, melodrama appears in the form of the hero plot, in which conflict is quickly established and the protagonist, with the aid of a few other supporting characters, takes action to resolve the conflict. Richard Carpenter discusses this ritualized television form:

Such a pattern, repeated night after night in dozens of versions, all portraying the same basic theme, implies that the TV audience derives satisfaction from a ritual formalization of ingrained feelings that the evil in the world can be overcome by men working together under the guidance of a leader. (In Sperry, 1981, p. 300)

When news events unfold over several days or weeks, two-minute "morality plays" become extended and melodramatic narrative forms can be developed. With the proliferation of network news stories concerning terrorism in the 1980s, analysis of this coverage provides the opportunity to investigate the themes or scenarios that might be communicated in sequences of related stories. Although many critics have noted the melodramatic nature of television news, scant detail has been given to the structure of discourse imposed by the logic of extended melodramatic narratives, or to the implications of using melodrama rather than other dramatic forms, such as satire or tragedy. Beginning then, with the components of news narratives about terrorism and the explanations of motive contained within them, this analysis explains the structure and rhetorical function of television news narratives about terrorism.

"FIXING" TERRORISM

The previous chapter explored ABC's tendency to obfuscate types of terroristic violence by portraying terrorism as a general phenomenon rather than as a conglomeration of discrete and situational actions. Treated as such, terrorism, as it appears in network newscasts, is nominalized; that is, the process of terrorist action has been transformed into a static condition or state of affairs. Simply put, nominalizations are abbreviated explanations created by casting verbs as noun phrases. In television news, words such as "terrorism" are treated as nominal conditions rather than processes, and audience (or reader) attention is directed to the present condition or event rather than to the circumstances or context that gave rise to the event.

Although nominalization is traditionally formulated as a linguistic technique, the degree to which audience attention is focused by the verbal syntax of broadcast news is difficult to assess. Nominalized reformulations undoubtedly occur in news presentations. For example, reporters often transfer blame from situations inciting protest to the actions of protesters, and although nominalization is often a necessary means of textual condensation, it is also used to present controversial assumptions as background knowledge for a reporter's claims. When applied to print news, nominalization is often analyzed according to the fixed or structural features of written text (for an example of a discourse analytic approach to newspaper accounts, see van Dijk, 1988). But when investigating televised news, the application of nominalization requires modification to account for the differences in written and spoken text.

The spoken words of anchors, correspondents, and interviewees can be transcribed, but fundamental differences between the structure of broadcast and print discourse mandate distinct strategies for analyzing the two types of text. Television's shorter length and dramatic structure of reports, its emphasis on visual material, the limitations of viewer control in reviewing televised information, and the simplification of news style to compensate for single-exposure viewing all differentiate the structure of television from print news. At a deeper level, the immediacy and presence of spoken language require adaptation of traditional linguistic approaches to discourse and narrative analysis. Television speaks in the present rather than in the inscribed past; in Ricoeur's (1976) terms, "singular identifications ultimately refer to the here and now determined by the interlocutionary situation" (p. 35).

Despite the transient nature of speech, television journalists, like those in print, need to form singular identifications, or nominalizations. But rather than occurring in the form of embedded noun phrases, nominalization arises from the creation of shared narrative forms and visual referents. The process of terrorism becomes a "situation perceived as common by the members of the dialogue":

In spoken discourse the ultimate criterion for the referential scope of what we say is the possibility of showing the thing referred to as a member of the situation common to both speaker and hearer. This situation surrounds the dialogue, and its landmarks can be shown by a gesture or by pointing a finger. (Ricoeur, 1976, p. 34)

Anchors and correspondents point to situations through visuals; viewers see situational surroundings in the film of news reports. Visual nominalizations, or static images used by the network to fix or identify events, become basic elements in the construction of the news story. They are a visual synecdoche, supplied by the news media and drawn from the audience's general understanding of an event.

Visual Nominalization

Several features of the visual environment are combined when news reports focus on one image to represent an event. A black and white photograph of Dozier shown for several consecutive nights during coverage of the story served as more than a referent to the living person; the image was also "culturally charged." As Turner (1988) explains in his description of film languages: "When we deal with images it is especially apparent that we are not only dealing with the object or the concept they represent, but we are also dealing with *the way in which they are represented*" (p. 45). Not only is the existence of a single image used to signify an event important, but the manner of presentation of that image also implies an attitude toward the event.

In the ABC News coverage of terrorism assessed here, nominalized images appeared in six of the nine terrorist events. Nominal images were those repeated throughout coverage of the event and appearing when an anchor or correspondent made a direct reference to the title given for the event. For instance, when Jennings referred to the "kidnapping of Brigadier General James Dozier," a photograph of Dozier appeared on the screen. Nominalized images reappeared in subsequent coverage of terrorism; when ABC News mentioned the kidnapping of Dozier during coverage of other terrorist actions, the same black and white photograph of Dozier was used to refer to the kidnapping.

The kidnapping of Dozier in December 1981 represented the first incident after Reagan's inauguration to be accompanied by a nominalized image. Although the hijacking of a Pakistani airliner in March 1981 amounted to, in Jennings' words, "the world's longest hijacking" (March 13, 1981), film acquired during the hijacking was not shown until the fifth day of coverage, and it consisted only of still shots, such as a black and white photograph of a Pakistan International Airlines jet, and graphics, such as a map of the region. During coverage of the hijacking, action sequences only occurred in special assignment reports on terrorism (which will be discussed in detail later) and in brief sequences depicting the activities of Pakistani authorities and hostage families.

In contrast, from the day of Dozier's abduction (Dec. 18, 1981), ABC News used a black and white photographed portrait of Dozier in military uniform to signify the event. This image was the only one of Dozier shown during the first week; other visuals were minimal and revolved around coverage of Dozier's wife. No other family members or friends were featured. Although ABC News later obtained photographs of Dozier holding Red Brigades' communiques, newscasts during the first 19 days of coverage, or until Dozier's release, consistently featured the first photograph.

This picture of Dozier differentiated the kidnapping from other terrorist events in several ways. Because the photograph was a portrait rather than a still image taken from an action sequence, there was no movement implied in the photograph. The picture was included not because it was taken during or was representative of the terrorist action, but because it depicted the person most affected by the incident. At this level of depiction, the photograph functions as formal identification. Dozier appeared in a close-up, frontal shot, dressed in military uniform and with an insignia visible on his lapel. The photograph thus accentuated Dozier's official duties in Italy and his position as a senior U.S. military officer attached to NATO. Although Dozier was "not considered a priority terrorist target" (Dec. 18, 1981), his status separated him from civilian targets of terrorism and therefore differentiated him from most viewers of the newscast. This emphasis of Dozier's military status helped keep the incident remote and impersonal, such that viewers would have been less likely to see terrorism as a potential threat to their own, civilian, welfare.

At a connotative level, the photograph personalized the kidnapping through expressive codes, which function as a truncated version of cultural codes for determining the subjective states of others. Expressive codes "can serve to amplify the personal qualities of the subject. These personal impressions are transferred to, and support, the ideological connotations of the whole story" (Hall, 1972, p. 68). Dozier's stern demeanor and barely perceptible smile complemented his military uniform. Although his face was highlighted by the tight framing of the picture, his expression lacked clear emotion and did not invite empathy. Consistent use of the black and white photograph personalized the abduction but also kept the drama distant with the focus on Dozier as a cool, professional, military official.

The bombing of U.S. Marine barracks in Beirut on October 23, 1983, also involved a military rather than civilian target. Repeated images consisted largely of depictions of the "grim search and rescue" (Oct. 23, 1983) following the attack; a mountain of concrete fragments filled most of the image, and soldiers picked through the smoking rubble. There was some variation in the scenes of the demolished building that were shown on ABC News, but all shots focused on the heap of concrete. The most common images, repeated during coverage of the bombing, in later coverage of terrorist incidents, and in network reviews of terrorism in the 1980s (see, for example, NBC's end-of-the-decade review, *The Eighties*), were from similar video clips taken during the first day of coverage. In ABC's representative image of the bombing, small groups of men walked along the top of the mound, creating clouds of white smoke as they extinguished remaining fires. In the foreground was a bent vertical flagpole; concrete rubble covered sections of a former barrier made of scattered tires and barbed wire fencing. Closer to the base of the heap and foregrounded in the image, metal debris could be distinguished from concrete, and a bulldozer sat to the right in the image. Soldiers paced along the edge of fencing and picked at the rubble with shovels. No one person's face was distinguishable, and some details were obscured by the gray and olive green tones that characterized most objects in the image.

Like the photograph of Dozier, nominalized images of the Beirut bombing associated that event with the U.S. military. Unlike the Dozier portrait, images of Beirut did not personalize the event. By focusing on the damage done to the barracks, the image may have diverted attention from the large loss of life resulting from the bombing. Of course, sequences surrounding the nominalized image included ample footage of rescue operations, but ABC News only used close or medium range shots of soldiers who were alive, or, if injured, were receiving medical attention. In addition, nominalization in the form of a destroyed building obscured the cause of the destruction, as similar images could be produced by natural disasters. This kind of nominalization was predictable, given the challenge to U.S. foreign policy posed by the bombing. Political violence, though fitting the formal news value of dramatic and vivid conflict, is problematic on an ideological level

because it signifies the world of politics as *it ought not to be*. It shows conflict in the system at its most extreme point. And this "breaches expectations" precisely because in our society conflict is supposed to be regulated, and politics is exactly "the continuation of social conflict without the resort to violence." (Hall, 1972, p. 70)

The nominalized images of the bombing of the Marine barracks in Beirut allowed us to remember the structural damage caused by terrorists without feeling personally threatened by terrorism and without calling attention to the political environment surrounding the action. To do so would be problematic, given the expectations of order and legitimacy held by most U.S. viewers.

When terrorists struck at civilian targets, opportunities for audience involvement in the incident increased. During the hijacking of TWA Flight 847, news networks gained access to video and audio tapes of hostages and their captors, adding movement and depth to the standardized image of a commercial airliner on a tarmac. On the first day of coverage, ABC opened the newscast with the TWA jet on approach at Beirut. Pilot John Testrake's transmission to air traffic control provided the voice-over: "He has pulled a hand grenade pin and he is ready to blow up the aircraft if he has to. We must—I repeat—we must land at Beirut" (June 14, 1985). As correspondent John Lawrence narrated the actions of the hijackers, visuals alternated between those of a plane in the air and on the tarmac and those of the Beirut airport. Lawrence's inclusion of the audio exchange between Testrake and the air traffic controller conveyed intensity otherwise absent from the still image of the plane; Testrake's vocal pitch and exasperation rose as he insisted that the hijackers' demands for refueling of the plane be met. "They are beating the passengers. They are beating the passengers. They are threatening to kill the passengers. They are threatening to kill them now. We want the fuel, *now. Immediately* "(June 14, 1985).

From the first day of coverage, the image of a TWA jet on a deserted tarmac carried an expressive level of connotation usually reserved for close-up, personalized shots or action sequences.

By the fifth day of the hijacking (June 19, 1985), a nominalized image of the plane on the tarmac was created based on ABC's exclusive interview with Testrake, conducted by Charles Glass as Testrake leaned out of the cockpit window. The interview opened with a close-up of the cockpit window on the left side of the plane. Testrake, with a fair complexion, gray hair, and in a white, short-sleeved shirt, was leaning out of the window, his left elbow and right hand resting on the window sill. Testrake briefly backed away from the open window; a hand wielding a pistol became visible on the left side of the window frame, followed by the face and shoulders of a dark, bearded man with short black hair. Waving his gun, the man shouted a few phrases to people on the tarmac. As he retreated into the cockpit to talk to Testrake, his gun was still visible as flashes of sunlight reflected off it. Testrake then leaned out of the window once again, folded his arms, and smiled. Darkened features of the gunman remained visible as he looked out of the cockpit from behind Testrake. This pose of Testrake, leaning out of the window as a dark, bearded man held a gun behind him, became the image most often repeated throughout coverage of the TWA hijacking.

Additional actions during the interview provided an immediate context for the nominalized image. Twice during the interview, the gunman interrupted a reporter's questioning by pulling Testrake away from the window. The gunman then leaned out of the cockpit, waving his pistol and shouting at the journalists. At one point, when a reporter asked Testrake a question about Israel's role in the hijacking, the gunman reached around Testrake with his left hand and covered Testrake's mouth, pulling him close to his body and striking the air with the pistol in his right hand. He then allowed Testrake to conclude the interview.

Both the waving gunman and the captive pilot came to symbolize the TWA Flight 847 hijacking in a still image that combined elements of civilian Americans as targets, commercial passenger jets as prisons, hostages as heroic, and dark, Islamic extremists as terrorists. Testrake's posture suggested a casual, even cavalier attitude; his grin showed bravado in the face of death, appearing in the form of the gunman watching from behind Testrake, brandishing the continuously visible pistol. Further, the audience's opportunity to see the airplane with both captive and captor combined with later coverage of Robert Stethem's dead body thrown from the plane turned the common jet into a vessel of terror rather than one of travel.

Finally, compositional features of the visual image added patriotic symbolism to the picture. Although the fuselage of the TWA jet was primarily white, the still image of Testrake was cropped such that below him were two red and white stripes running horizontally along the bottom of the frame. In the lower left corner was a wedge of navy blue, created by a black strip along the bottom edge of the jet's windscreen that glistened as a dark blue in the sunlight. The visual effect simulated that of a U.S. flag, on which Testrake rested his arms and behind which the terrorist loomed.

Nominalized images also appeared during the *Achille Lauro* hijacking and the massacres at the Rome and Vienna airports, but they were based on events occurring over a relatively short period of time (one to three days). On ABC's first day of news coverage in the hijacking of the Italian cruise ship, the *Achille Lauro*, the newscast opened by showing a full-length, color photograph of the blue and white ship (Oct. 7, 1985). Throughout the three days, ABC News used variations of this picture; once a black and white photograph taken from above the cruise liner was shown, and at other times a video camera panned the length of the hull, circling around the bow and stopping so that the name, *Achille Lauro*, was visible. Despite file footage of terrorist groups used in background reports and interviews with relatives of the passengers on board, images of the ship dominated during explanations of the event. Somewhat ironically, ABC's Hall Walker criticized Italian news coverage for providing only file images of the vessel; this file footage was the same as that used by ABC News.

On October 9, 1985, when speculation began about the death of Leon Klinghoffer, ABC News showed two photographs of him, and the next day his widow, Marilyn Klinghoffer, provided another opportunity for a personalized image of the hijacking. The Klinghoffers served as a visual focus of the event, but they did not come to stand for it, perhaps due to a combination of the paucity of available pictures showing Leon Klinghoffer shortly before his death, the continuing news focus on the *Achille Lauro* hijackers after their departure from the ship, and the ease of both verbal and visual identification afforded by the picture of the blue hull and white lettering that read "Achille Lauro." Nominalization in the form of the cruise ship itself served as a reminder that terrorists strike at vacationers, and that places of recreation can become places of terror.

The intensity of images of terrorist attacks on holiday travelers peaked with news coverage of the shooting massacres at the Rome and Vienna airports. This time, journalists had immediate access to footage of the carnage; visuals were more varied and more graphic. ABC opened its December 27, 1985, newscasts with a close-up, still image of the face and chest of a man lying on a floor; his lips were parted and sunglasses covered his eyes. The camera zoomed out to include four more bodies sprawled on the floor and tagged as police exhibits. This image froze and shrunk to the lower right corner of the television screen; action continued in a second inserted frame in the upper right corner. Here, the camera panned a tile floor splattered with blood and stopped at a group of abandoned suitcases. These two images came to represent the Rome and Vienna airport massacres, and the picture of five dead travelers scattered and tagged on the floor of the Rome airport came to represent the bloodier of the attacks.

The shot of the five bodies appeared with some variations in the newscasts. For instance, in one brief sequence a man appeared and covered the middle body with a yellow tarp; in another, the camera zoomed to the three bodies in the center of the frame. All versions, however, shared essential characteristics. First, the setting was obviously one of a busy airport; the bodies were surrounded by luggage and snack bar furnishings, such as a linoleum counter to the right, and small, round snack tables to the left. Second, exhibit tags were visible on the bodies, suggesting recent death caused by a criminal action. Third, the bodies were clearly those of civilians, and their clothing was casual and ordinary. Men and women were dressed in dark slacks, light shirts and cardigans or light-weight jackets. Fourth, the shots were taken from above the scene in a manner of surveillance, similar to the visual record taken by police or other authorities. Finally, the positions of the bodies and their visible wounds denoted violent and sudden death. For instance, person "A," to the left of the image, lay on his back, his head tilted sideways and resting on the metal base of a snack table. In closer shots, a crumpled napkin was visible next to his right hand. Person "B" lay face up, arms outstretched and legs twisted to the left.

These images of death were the most graphic of the nominalizations used to represent terrorist actions. Although the visuals gave few clues about the time or region of the attack or the terrorist group thought to be responsible, they conveyed the random and indiscriminate nature of terrorist violence. Unlike the kidnapping of Dozier, who was a military target, and the bombing of the Marine barracks in Beirut, where visual emphasis was on structural rather than human loss, images of the airport attacks focused explicitly on the deaths of civilians. Further, like nominalizations of the TWA Flight 847 and the *Achille Lauro* hijackings, the Rome airport massacre exemplified a focus of terrorist attacks on transportation industries in general and, more specifically, on vacation travelers. As news coverage of terrorism increased, so did nominalizations based on images that offered increasing opportunities for viewer identification and perceptions of personal threat and terror.

Fighting Images: Protagonists as Paper Tigers

Nominalization, as a process of visual condensation, provides narrators and audiences with a visible, symbolic referent for specific terrorist action. Like ideographs, nominalized images simplify and mystify; they function synecdochically, condensing problems "into a few shots that then displace actual time and space considerations in order to forward the narrative structure" (Medhurst, 1989, p. 186), and they are integral to the development of a structural frame for network news portrayals of terrorism. Although synecdoche allows for movement between representation and context, nominalization can discourage this check between the image and the environment from which it is drawn. Nominalized images form a basis for reaction rather than reflection; functioning as condensational symbols, they evoke emotions associated with the situation. As part of an ongoing narrative, nominalized images serve as a statement of the terrorist problem, and television news depicts U.S. government officials as responding to terrorist actions on the basis of the understanding of terrorism implicit in the nominalized images.

With his inauguration in 1981, Reagan assumed the role of protagonist in fighting terrorism, pledging "swift and resolute" action against terrorists. Events over the next four years, however, did not result in the type of action Reagan promised. ABC News consistently highlighted the disparity between pledges made by the Reagan administration and the subsequent failure of quick resolution, posing Reagan as a paper tiger and thus risking a lack of narrative closure implicit in a hero quest.

Although the March 1981 hijacking of a Pakistani airplane was predominantly an internal dilemma for Pakistan—it involved followers of the late Pakistani Prime Minister Zulfikar Ali Bhutto and the Pakistan government, it was resolved by the Pakistan government meeting the hijackers' demands for the release of political prisoners, and it included only three U.S. passengers who happened to be on board—the incident allowed Reagan to repeat his proclamations about the compelling need for "the world" to "find a way to deal with terrorists" (March 13, 1981). Similarly, at the outset of the Dozier kidnapping, Reagan expressed his outrage:

They are cowardly bums. They aren't heroes, or they don't have a cause that justifies what they're doing. They're cowards. They wouldn't have the guts to stand up to anyone individually in a fis— in any kind of a fair contest. (Dec. 18, 1981)

Reagan's "slip of the tongue" helped establish the hero/villain duality and reified his role as protagonist, as the hero in the white hat challenging the villain to abide by the rules of fair fighting.

ABC News replayed Reagan's challenge at various points, but news correspondents noted that an incident such as the Dozier kidnapping was "a very different situation, of course, from the Iran hostage crisis that ended as President Reagan took office, permitting him to make a stern warning to any future terrorist kidnappers." ABC's David Ensor responded to Reagan's warning of "swift and effective retribution" with the comment: "But the Dozier case does not lend itself to swift and effective action. The president is obligated to wait and watch" (Dec. 27, 1981). When Dozier was finally released, ABC News granted credit to the Italian police who rescued him; although "in one sense" the United States had "finally won one, the general's freedom was specifically won by Italian anti-terrorist police" (Jan. 28, 1982). After praising the "textbook rescue operation" conducted by the Italians, Jennings reminded viewers of the danger still posed by the "purveyors of violence" who had "waged an unremitting campaign" to "destroy existing democratic institutions" without a "coherent vision of the future. For theirs is the power to destroy, not to build" (Jan. 28, 1982). Victory over terrorism was credited to the Italians and would provide only short-term respite.

As coverage of terrorism intensified during the 1980s, so did coverage of Reagan's rhetoric and failure of overt action. Reagan was described as reacting to the bombing of the Marine barracks with "horror, outrage, and frustration at not being able to immediately get at the perpetrators of the act" (Oct. 23, 1983). Although U.S. officials "talked as though they might retaliate, they never did," promising instead that "future terrorist acts directed at Americans will draw an immediate military response from the U.S." (Nov. 28, 1983).

But future terrorist acts did not lead to the promised response. The hijacking of TWA Flight 847 put "a very powerful nation" in "a very difficult position." Although Reagan "came to office talking tough about terrorism" and said he would "hit hard at terrorists," his "deeds have not matched his words" (June 14, 1985; June 18, 1985). As the hijacking continued, the president was noted to "promise stern measures," but "except for appointing Vice President Bush to head a task force to consider how to best combat terrorism, that was it" (June 20, 1985). On the eighth day of coverage, Sam Donaldson summarized the administration's position:

The feeling here is one of impotence. They're on the dime. Nothing has been able to be done to try and free the hostages, because officials here will not deal with them publicly, will not ask Israel publicly, or privately for that matter, to release those Shi'ite prisoners, and so the situation is simply status quo. (June 21, 1985)

The administration not only failed to retaliate as promised, but also failed to attempt a negotiated resolution to the problem.

As Reagan continued to threaten the hijackers, ABC News continued to challenge the willingness of the administration to fulfill those threats. The administration's call for a military blockade was described as "tough talk" by Donaldson, and correspondent Charles Glass devoted a news segment to detailing the futility of the administration's new plans (June 25, 1985). Resolution of the crisis rested primarily with Nabih Berri, the Shi'ite negotiator, who would not arrange the release of the hostages until he received "a guarantee from Washington that it [would] not attack Lebanon." This condition arose only after Reagan temporarily sabotaged Berri's efforts with more "tough talk." Correspondent Don Kladstrup explained: "The feeling here is that if President Reagan hadn't said the things he did about the hijackers, calling them thugs, barbarians, and murderers, that the hostages might very well have been gone by now" (June 29, 1985).

Despite these and other criticisms of the administration's rhetoric, following the hostage release Reagan continued this type of talk as his primary form of public action in response to terrorism. Donaldson discussed the escalation of intensity in Reagan's rhetoric following the release of the TWA Flight 847 passengers:

White House officials insist that the president's tough talk is not just bluster, that the political commentators who were pointing out the Reagan presidency has been marked with much bark and little bite have got it wrong this time, that the president knows in talking so tough he is raising the stakes not only on terrorism, but on his own credibility. And that tough talk will be backed up with action. (July 8, 1985)

While statements from the White House built expectations of overt action, ABC News challenged the credibility of those expectations, implying that words needed to be followed with action.

By the time of the October 7, 1985, hijacking of the *Achille Lauro*, the assumption of an ineffective protagonist informed the earliest presentations of the incident. According to ABC News, the administration tried to "downplay" the hijacking: "At the State Department, they wouldn't even repeat standing U.S. policy against dealing with the hijackers." Official comment could not be obtained, because "they're working hard behind the scenes with other governments to deal with this emergency, and high-profile comment would reduce their ability to do so. *It would also further spotlight their impotence if they can't*" (Oct. 8, 1985; emphasis added). Eventually, the administration did take action in the form of forcing an Egyptian plane carrying the hijackers to land in Italy, where the four hijackers and two Palestinian officials on board the plane, Hani Hasan and Mohammad Abbas Zaida, were taken into custody by the Italian police.

This "dramatic military mission" received some praise in news reports, as correspondents talked of "finally winning one" and of the need for a "country so battered and bruised by terrorism, so frustrated by its unpunished madness and murder" to see "some evidence that terrorists cannot operate with impunity" (Oct. 11, 1985). But this ecstasy faded quickly as Italy allowed the leader of the operation, Abbas, to leave the country. The administration had invested "enormous prestige" in "bringing a man it calls a terrorist to justice" but was unable to do so (Oct. 13, 1985). On October 14, ABC News reported: "There is growing recognition that Abbas has slipped out of America's grasp, and to continue to extradite him in an unsuccessful campaign makes the U.S. once again appear helpless, just three days after its most impressive victory against terrorism" (Oct. 14, 1985). Attempts to capture Abbas continued to fail, and ABC News returned the administration to its status as paper tiger.

By the end of 1985, when terrorists killed 16 people at the El Al ticket counters in the Rome and Vienna airports, the sufficiency of public statements as action had been strained to its limit. Criticism of public statements can be predicted based on two requirements of the narrative. First, television anchors and correspondents, as objective and omniscient narrators, are expected to challenge the viability of public statements. Second, criticism could be expected when the protagonist does not take the overt action demanded by melodrama. Television narratives require constant movement toward resolution. Although criticism of public officials provides dramatic tension and enhances the watchdog status of a news organization, it does not sustain momentum. This does not pose a problem if the problem is based on events that are continuous and outside public scrutiny, as in more routine happenings such as congressional hearings. But in a situation where audience attention is focused, the network cannot afford to drop the story. Momentum must be sustained.

Neither the administration nor ABC News could afford to have the narrative fail. For the administration, putting the teeth back into the tiger would require overt military action. For ABC News, saving the narrative required sustaining momentum in the story of terrorism until a suitable protagonist brought temporary closure through resolution. One way that television journalists compensate for an ineffective protagonist is by assuming the role of protagonist themselves. For instance, journalists can create and then report about an event that keeps a news story moving. Or, increasingly, journalists serve as television diplomats and thus become key figures in the unfolding drama.

ABC News coverage of the 1985 TWA Flight 847 hijacking contained examples of both conventions. On June 19, the newscast opened with an exclusive interview of the TWA flight crew. Of course, there was little the crew could say, and their comments about adjusting to Lebanese food hardly constituted a newsworthy event. But the footage of the captured flight crew was certainly dramatic, and ABC's orchestration of exclusive interviews justified continuing the hijacking as the lead story on the evening news, despite the lack of change in the condition of the hostages.

Perhaps more troubling is the movement of media personalities into the narrative rather than their remaining outside it in the traditional narrator role. Jennings played a negotiator, asking Israeli Ambassador Benjamin Netanyahu if he would meet the terrorists' demands; Glass asked the pilot of the plane, Captain Testrake, if a rescue operation was feasible; and Glass provided an ineffective CIA with taped information about terrorist activity on the plane, information the CIA should have been able to get on its own. Asking questions of the Shi'ites (e.g., "If you were convinced the Israelis were going to release the Lebanese Shi'ites tomorrow, would you release the passengers today?") simulated a bargaining setting, asking participants in the conflict the conditions under which they would act. With this format, the anchor becomes a negotiator; the network becomes an advisory board for foreign policy.

This role taken by journalists, and, more generally, television news, moves delicate negotiations into a public forum. The trend toward media diplomacy began during coverage of the Iranian hostage crisis of 1979–80. Although some journalists recognized the central role of television in international communication at this time, they also saw their role as that of neutral observer (Altheide, 1981) rather than active participant. Since television is structured largely by the melodramatic narrative, the options for presenting negotiations are limited, and they inevitably are fit into the bifurcated world of good and evil. Even the visual nature of television news creates constraints; news producers can't "show" negotiations, but they can show an exchange of statements. Diplomacy by television journalists doesn't allow subtlety or flexibility, and it greatly limits the ability of either side in a conflict to negotiate. Television can help make the entire process look useless.

Television journalists step into narratives in other ways as well. To create action, news narratives also rely on passivation, evident in the video postcard, and presupposition, which helps journalists build contexts and suggest responses to foreign conflict.

MOBILIZED EMOTIONS AND THE VIDEO POSTCARD

In television news, viewers are invited to feel frustration through the lives of those people most affected by it: the victims and their families, who become focal points in the narratives through the process of passivation. Like nominalization, passivation in the ABC newscasts relied on the dualities present in ideographs. In this instance, the ideograph of America provided a characterization of the U.S. citizen as a target of terrorists. Through passivation, which places the person affected by a process in the position of subject rather than object, narratives place emphasis on participants rather than on the causes or agents of a process. In network news accounts of terrorism, a focus on those affected by terrorist acts of violence engages the empathetic emotions of viewers.

Television news coverage of the families affected by terrorism has been emphasized at least since the 1979 capture of the U.S. Embassy in Iran. ABC News included reports on the families affected by terrorism in coverage of all terrorist acts included in this analysis, with some variation in the frequency, nature, and point at which the reports were first used. The amount of coverage of hostages and their families peaked for all three networks during the hijacking of TWA Flight 847; footage of friends and families constituted 30 percent of ABC's nightly news coverage of the hijacking (Elliott, 1988).

Journalists justify these extensive reports on the basis of news value. Lee Hockstader of the *Washington Post* explains:

I think that one of the fundamental tenets of journalism is explaining to a great mass of people . . . what other people are doing and what's happening to other people. . . . It's a tradition in journalism and simply a response to natural human emotion to want to know how those other people felt about what happened to them or their friends. (In Elliott, 1988, p. 68)

ABC News described hostages and their families as ordinary people we "can identify with" and check in with each night to, as Donaldson put it, "see how the families are bearing up." The following section illustrates that as victims and their families become components in a plot sequence, their accounts provide movement where none might otherwise exist. By highlighting hostages and families as affected agents and making their private ordeal public, ABC News accomplished the dual task of both involving viewers in the drama by engaging their emotions and of portraying the network as serving a vital social function.

Video Postcards

In coverage of any tragedy, journalists present the experiences and feelings of victims and their loved ones. In some situations, reporters act as messengers of bad news, as happened when, hours before Navy officials arrived to tell the Stethems that their son had been killed, news teams set up cameras outside the Stethems' home in anticipation of recording their reaction to the impending notification.

When hostages or prisoners are taken, coverage extends beyond the immediate reactions of the families of victims to the sending of "video postcards" through the news media. Video postcards are testimonials, often containing greetings, statements about health, or prayers for freedom, that are made by hostages and directed to their families and the public, or by friends and families and directed to the hostages and governments involved in the situation. Video postcards give the illusion of direct communication between hostages and their families while also focusing on personal tragedy.

Although three Americans were held on board an aircraft in the Pakistani hijacking of March 1981, the identities of the passengers were not determined until after the hijackers surrendered, and thus video postcards could not be used. But with the TWA hijacking in June 1985, video postcards became standard features in ABC News presentations of terrorism. On June 14, the first day of coverage, Jennings introduced the postcards, using the semantic frame of the victim supplied by the American ideograph: "With more than 100 Americans on board the hijacked plane, there are, as you can imagine, a good many relatives waiting anxiously in this country for news. Among them, the friends and relatives of religious pilgrims from suburban Chicago." Correspondent Joe Spencer began his report with footage from St. Margaret Mary's Church in Algonquin, Illinois, where parishioners expressed their horror about the hijacking. Next, Spencer switched scenes to a living room, where "hostage families cluster around the television, hanging on to each new piece of news." They would spend the night "waiting at home, praying for the travelers' lives" (June 14, 1985). As the hijacking continued, families "willingly opened" their living rooms "to share their ordeal with the whole nation" (June 29, 1985).

Coverage of the hostage families continued daily throughout the hijacking of TWA Flight 847. In addition to interviewing relatives of the hostages about their "emotional roller coaster" as they were caught in "deepening madness" (June 20, 1985), ABC News solicited opinions from them about Reagan's performance and used these opinions to build generalizations about public sentiment. Wooten opened one of his reports this way: "Across the nation, the crackle of America's voice. And from this mass of personal sentiment, a sense of a country emerges" (June 18, 1985). Of course, rather than rising organically from a consensual public view, the "sense of a country" was shaped directly by ABC's choice of sound bites:

> Burt Schmarak: I think we ought to negotiate like crazy, and then when negotiations are over, retaliate in a very severe kind.
>
> Andrew Apicella: If you retaliate in kind, you're going to get it back twice as much.
>
> Margaret Busby: But if you just give in, you're giving others the chance to do the same thing, knowing that they're going to get away with it.
>
> James Brockwood: They've got an aircraft carrier out there, they've got 1,500 Marines waiting. Send 'em on in, nobody else is gonna do the job for us.

Elaine Blumenthal: I'm not real sure what to do, 'cause I don't know a lot about foreign policy. But I sure do think we ought to be able to do more than we're doing. (June 18, 1985)

The "sense of a country" implied in this exchange was one of frustration and desire for military retaliation. The objection voiced early in the sequence was quickly dismissed, and a military option was given credibility due to the information provided by Brockwood.

A similar exchange was aired during coverage of the *Achille Lauro* hijacking later that year. Kladstrup described these unnamed women as "profoundly frustrated":

A: I think my government should put their best efforts forward so that this stops, once and for all.

B: So you're telling, you're saying that our present administration is not taking the proper steps in times like this.

A: I'm not—

B: What do you propose, then? That's what I'm asking.

A: [We've] got to have some rules that everyone has to follow. And I believe in violence if it's necessary. I really do.

B: I don't believe in violence, because if we have violence, we're going to take an incident and you'll have a world catastrophe. I mean, something should be done.

A: We shouldn't have to be afraid of when we leave our country, that this is going to happen to us. How much longer can this keep going on? That this small group of people can scare the living daylights out of everyone. (Oct. 8, 1985)

Both women agreed that "something should be done"; they expressed anger and resentment, and the segment opened and closed with the suggestion of retaliation. In voicing dissatisfaction with past government actions against terrorism, the women offered testimony in relation to a theme introduced in the newscasts. The interviews provided emotional and moral proof for the thesis of incompetency and increased the status of the narrator. Also, whether by accident or by design, the public sentiment portrayed fit with the expectations created by a narrative structure that promises overt action taken by a hero.

In addition to airing public frustrations during terrorist attacks involving hostages, ABC News contrasted the ordinary nature of people involved with the special status conferred on them due to circumstance, implying that any American could become a victim. Shortly after news of the *Achille Lauro* hijacking was released, Sherr interviewed the families of those Americans on board the ship:

Correspondent Lynn Sherr: For the families of at least ten more Americans, the worst agony was in knowing for sure, knowing that this time it is their relatives who are hostages.

Lisa Klinghoffer: I still don't know, except that the fact that I'm terrified. I just can't believe it could happen to us.

Steve Hodes: We've always felt sympathy towards the relatives of the—of the victims of terrorism. But certainly we didn't expect it to be—essentially a victim myself, or have my family victimized.

Sherr: There are no rules of behavior for hostage families, but one member of this rapidly growing group has her own message for this particular moment of terror.

Carol Hodes: I really wish that the hijackers would take into consideration that these are, these are not good hostages for them. They're not—they should be let go, they're not healthy, and they're—every one of them is over 65, and it really would be a [good] thing for them to do, to let those people go. (Oct. 8, 1985)

As relatives of the hostages made their pleas to terrorists and voiced their incredulity, and as the murder of Leon Klinghoffer, an "elderly, crippled gentleman" (Oct. 10, 1985) was revealed, it became apparent that no American was safe from terrorism.

Video postcards draw viewers into drama by personalizing tragedy. Hostage families show their range of emotions, voice their opinions and frustrations, and appear as ordinary people caught in an incomprehensible situation. Additionally, as coverage of terrorism continued, the pool of characters playing the role of victim expanded, forming a corps of experts by virtue of personal experience. An example comes from coverage of the *Achille Lauro* hijacking, with a report on the former TWA Flight 847 hostages "watching those new hostages on TV from back in Illinois, and taking it very personally. . . . They knew what it was like for the Americans on the ship. The fear, the hate" (Oct. 11, 1985). Once people had been victimized by terrorists, they became a community through shared experience and part of the resources from which journalists drew in their depictions of personal tragedy.

Finally, video postcards also create a sense of community by providing a channel of communication between hostages and their families. During the hijacking of TWA Flight 847, postcards from hostages became a common feature of ABC's news coverage:

Arthur Toga: I miss my wife very much. I want to go home. I want to go home to my family and my friends. I am healthy and being taken care of, but I want to go home very bad.

Richard Herzberg: I'm alive and well, living in Beirut. I'd like to say hello to my wife Suzie and my parents, and tell them that everything here could be better, but I'm fine and we will be out very soon.

Robert Trautmann: Hi. I'm Bob Trautmann. I'd just like to say hello to my family and my wife, Eva, and my kids, Ashley and Catherine. Just want to tell everybody that I'm fine, we're being treated okay. I want to get out of here though, and I hope to be home very shortly.

Ralf Traugott: Hostage Ralf Traugott. Hello, everybody, especially Nicky. I'm healthy, I feel strong inside and outside. Please write letters to Congress and the president. Hope to see you all soon. (June 20, 1985)

Regardless of the probable pressure placed on the hostages during filming, the resulting postcards fit the standard format of the video greeting that appears in countless television programs, such as the "hello" of a *Wheel of Fortune* contestant to his or her children. But in the case of ABC News coverage, viewers were privy not just to the emotions of those affected by terrorism, but also to the conversations between hostages and their families. In extended terrorist incidents such as the TWA Flight 847 hijacking, this focus on the affected participants through the video postcard gave movement to the narrative, as interviews with the hostages became the lead news events in coverage of the hijacking (June 19, 20, 24, 27, 28; July 1, 4, 1985). Video postcards thus constituted a key element in shaping both the terms and movement of the narrative.

Helping the Hostages: ABC as Benefactor

Continual presentations of video postcards left ABC News open to charges of exploitation of hostages and complicity with terrorist aims. ABC News responded to these charges in at least two ways: first, by showing public reliance on the media for news of friends and family, and second, by promoting the public service performed by the network in uniting hostages and their families.

Throughout coverage of terrorist actions, ABC inserted comments into newscasts about the need of the public to turn to the network for information about friends and relatives. In the March 1981 hijacking of a jet in Pakistan, Pakistanis learned of the hostage release through the news media: "Even families and friends of the hostages had to rely on press reports to know that their wait was almost over" (March 15, 1985). News reports did more than give the status of victims; according to some hostages, news media also functioned as a support system. As released hostage James Palmer said, "The greatest thing that the hostages can see is when we look at the newspapers and listen to the radio, that the American people are behind us, saying bring us home. As long as that continues, the hostages will continue their high morale" (June 16, 1985). News broadcasts were thus presented as an essential element for the well-being of hostages.

ABC News also claimed to provide vital emotional support to the families of hostages by providing "video reunions" (June 19 and 26, 1985) to families who "take some desperate comfort at least from these brief glimpses of husbands and fathers, brothers and sons" (June 20, 1985). Although all three networks used video postcards, ABC News claimed special status from "exclusive interviews" with hostages (e.g., June 19, 20, 27, 1985) and, at times, implied that victims preferred ABC News as the forum in which to express themselves:

[The bombing of] TWA Flight 840 created a personal tragedy, a pain worse than most of us will ever be asked to bear. . . . [Survivors] have avoided the public and journalists. But now, they are ready to tell Americans how they feel and decided to do it through ABC News. (April 6, 1986)

Far from exploiting those affected by terrorists, ABC News represented itself as providing them with a needed service. Families were "relieved" when they saw the postcards and said that "it's a big help" to see the hostages (June 24, 1985). Given the visible trauma that hostages and their families experienced, providing them with a video connection allowed ABC News to claim the role of benefactor while simultaneously building the emotional intensity of the narrative.

The ABC News focus on the continual agony of hostage families combined with portrayals of government impotence played on the public frustration and humiliation associated with terrorism. In addition, the narrative frame in which events were placed further frustrated viewers, because the structure of the news stories led viewers to expect the emotional congruence found in melodrama. This mobilization of emotion put the viewer in a prime position to accept responsive action that fit the expectations built by the logic of narrative form.

BUILDING CONTEXTS AND SUGGESTING RESPONSES

News reports contain countless assumptions about the nature of events and the world that creates them. The background assumptions in a journalist's statements form presuppositions, or embedded claims that provide a narrative context into which individual events are placed. When main claims seem reasonable, embedded presuppositions such as societal values are more difficult to discern. Presuppositions effect closure in interpretations, because they remain as generally held assumptions even when the specific event on which the assumption is based challenges those presuppositions.

Analysis of presuppositions provides an entry point for determining the implicit values in news narratives. Most statements made by television reporters contain some kind of presupposition that is based on journalistic experience or prior news reports. For instance, when Jennings began coverage of TWA Flight 847 with the lead, "The hijackers widen their war in the Middle East," he presupposed that a constant, identifiable group of hijackers (*the* hijackers) was continuing past activities and that a state of war existed (June 14, 1985). For his statement to be credible, Jennings had to draw from assumptions that he and his viewers shared and that had become part of a symbolic narrative about terrorism. This conventional wisdom existed both outside the newscast, in the form of semantic frames such as ideographs, and inside the newscast, in the form of background reports that provided contexts for news events. The degree to which network news contextualizes events is questionable, as evidenced by the practice of treating terrorism as a phenomenon rather than as a response to political conflict and by the nominalization of terrorist events. Nonetheless, some kinds of shared assumptions must be built between the teller of the narrative and the audience who listens. In a general sense, audiences derive these assumptions from the symbolic narrative framework into which events are fit. At a more specific level, audiences must be persuaded to make the judgment that a particular news event fits the larger narrative.

The credibility of presuppositions depends on the fit between the immediate event and the narrative as reconstructed in the newscast. ABC News needed to represent the widened "war in the Middle East" in a manner that warranted specific presuppositions. One way to construct a narrative context is by using the anchor to establish the terms by which audiences understand an event. But individual reports, which are more often structured as narratives internal to the newscast, may carry more influence than the flippant, "interpretive" comments made by news anchors. Particularly when a story is new or unfamiliar to viewers, as with remote terrorist actions, viewers may not have a context in which to place the news item. As Lewis (1985) explains in his analysis of the structure of newscasts, "The ability to absorb the item's introduction into a reading is fairly dependent upon the decoder *already knowing* about the narrative context to which the introduction refers." Without access to this narrative context, "the broadcaster's meaning [is] *simply not communicated*" (p. 211). Background reports and special assignment series are thus instrumental in providing viewers with characterizations of terrorists or with contexts by which they can interpret unfolding news accounts of terrorism. Based on these characterizations and the narrative construction in which they appear, news reports promulgate embedded assumptions about the appropriateness of various responses to terrorism.

The Language of Speculation and the Language of Strength

Network news operates on the pretense that it presents facts; ABC News reports hard news, or news that is timely and relevant and can be verified or documented. Schudson (1986) writes that "the journalist's minimal obligation is not to help the reader understand but to *get it right*," and the ideology of U.S. journalism mandates that "reporters report and do not interpret" (pp. 105–6). But in the pursuit of making events meaningful to viewers, journalists must interpret events. One means of attaching significance to an event is through speculation, where stories "do not deal with what is but with what might be" (p. 106). Using the language of speculation, reporters tell stories that are not yet newsworthy but are likely to become so. Through the power of suggestion, journalists set expectations about the direction of the narrative.

In initial coverage of terrorism during the Reagan presidency, and again during the administration's renewal of vows against terrorism in early 1986, ABC News used a language of speculation to establish assumptions about the manner with which the U.S. government must deal with terrorism. This speculation also established the presuppositions that followed in the emergent language of strength. Beginning with ABC's coverage of the Pakistani hijacking in March 1981, McWethy presented a special assignment series on terrorism that provided a context for terrorist violence by which the hijacking could be understood. This special assignment series also featured scenarios of actions terrorists *might* take, such as seizing control of the Panama Canal or bombing a Democratic convention, whereby "half the political leaders in the country would become hostages or worse" (March 13, 1981). Stating what might happen is itself a form of presupposition, for it assumes knowledge about the motivations and predictability of actors. For instance, the statement that "international terrorists have been planning to step up their attacks on NATO targets" (Dec. 21, 1981) assumed a range of activities far beyond that of the Red Brigades taking its first non-Italian hostage.

Perhaps more importantly, speculation creates a sense of urgency. "A story about what failed to happen over the past several years is really a story about what may happen in the years to come if some action is not taken" (Schudson, 1986, p. 107). ABC News covered the activities of people preparing for future terrorist actions. "What if" stories included segments on the growth of private security businesses (July 2, 1985; Jan. 16, 1986) and airline safety programs (June 24, 1985). With each speculation came the remedy for catastrophe in the form of military action. For instance, ABC News created the following scenario for a possible terrorist attack in Panama:

Navy patrol boats monitor the harbor and canal. Crack troops specially trained in counter-terrorist warfare are called in, fighting guerrillas in the jungle, using their own hit-and-run tactics. An AC-130 gunship, a lethal night-fighter, cruises overhead. This type of plane was to be part of the Iran rescue mission if the Delta team had ever reached Tehran. Its job, in a terrorist situation: lay down a deadly blanket of fire with pinpoint accuracy. . . . If hostages were taken [at the U.S. Embassy in Panama], elements of the super-secret Delta rescue team would be dispatched. (March 13, 1981)

As McWethy narrated the sequence of events, corresponding visuals verified the power of the military. U.S. soldiers were flown in by helicopter to fight in jungle warfare. The technological prowess of a war plane was suggested by an interior shot of its control panel and a demonstration of the plane firing at night. And ABC News implied that, had President Carter allowed *these* forces to carry out a rescue mission rather than opting for the attempt that failed, the hostages in Tehran would have been freed.

Following this sequence, ABC News presented terrorism expert Robert Kupperman, who challenged the viability of using military force: "You know, the primary way of fighting terrorism is not with rescue squads, it's not with real advanced technology. It's with good intelligence" (March 13, 1981). McWethy used the issue of intelligence as a transition, leaving his prior emphasis on military solutions to stand on the basis of his presentation, which was far more compelling than Kupperman's sound bite.

As challenges to the administration's competence increased, so did speculation about military reprisals. Among the responses to the bombing of the Marine barracks in Beirut, the Pentagon was shown to be considering "allowing the Marines to more aggressively deal with threats. . . . It might also mean a quicker, more brutal response to the attacks" (Oct. 24, 1983). The capacity of the Marines to react effectively was assumed, based on ample depictions of "America's

military option," exemplified in this report aired during the hijacking of TWA
Flight 847:

The nuclear-powered aircraft carrier, *USS Nimitz*, accompanied by other warships, including
the cruiser *South Carolina* and a guided missile destroyer *Kid*, shouldered into position today
off the coast of Lebanon, the *Kid* so close it could be observed from the control tower at
Beirut airport. It was a show of sea and air strength by the U.S. Sixth Fleet. More importantly,
it provided what experts said would be a base for a rescue, or retaliation. At the same time,
the *USS Spartan* and other ships in the Mediterranean amphibious force headed methodically
eastward. . . . Navy officials acknowledge the amphibious force could be used to secure the
beach for a military mission. That mission could be carried out by elite commandoes known
as the Delta Force. (June 17, 1985)

Although correspondent Dean Reynolds concluded that "the military option will
be secondary" as long as "there appear to be somewhat useful negotiations underway to free the hostages," visual simulations of military exercises supported the
presupposition that a rescue could be accomplished.

Each mention of "the military option" carried the assumption that retaliation was
an effective and thus desirable response to terrorism. Although Reagan had publicly
"ruled out the use of force," U.S. military vessels were depicted as ready to respond.
Glass reminded viewers that "out at sea . . . are American ships of the Sixth Fleet,
brought in during this hostage crisis. Among the flotilla were the helicopter
transport, the amphibious landing craft *Spartan*, and the guided missile cruiser
South Carolina" (June 23, 1985). ABC News touted the strength of these forces as
internationally acknowledged; even "Lebanese Shi'ites are aware of what those
ships and jet fighters can do" (June 25, 1985).

In the absence of overt military action taken during terrorist incidents, ABC
News needed to reinforce the credibility of its own presuppositions, and repeatedly
did so in background reports. Correspondent Jack Smith detailed "the military
option" this way:

There are American soldiers, the military special operations forces trained to rescue hostages
from terrorists, and under the Reagan administration they've undergone an unprecedented
peacetime build-up. Manpower is up 30 percent, and the special operations budget has tripled
to make these men a real alternative to conventional forces or nuclear weapons. . . . Delta
Force is the Army's elite commando team, several hundred of them trained specifically to
kill terrorists and free their captives. . . . The Navy, too, has its SEALS, or sea, air, and land
soldiers; they are expert at swimming ashore undetected and are trained in counterterrorism.
(June 27, 1985)

Smith then mentioned past failures of U.S. rescue operations and the difficulties in
using special forces in the TWA Flight 847 hijacking. Dramatic visuals, however,
again supported the credibility of the military. Department of Defense simulations
showed soldiers freeing families from barren buildings and escorting them to
waiting helicopters, firing M-16s and pistols as they stormed hallways and climbing

out of swamps with rifles ready for combat. Although the administration's "cherished commandoes cannot be used" during the hijacking (June 27, 1985), ABC News suggested that U.S. military forces were ready to respond to the next terrorist action.

Finally, military retaliation was contrasted with negotiation as an option for action, a dichotomy that posed a false dilemma that was continually reinforced in news coverage of terrorism. Both negotiation, in which the administration vowed not to engage, and retaliation, presented as its sole alternative, were short-term reactions rather than reflections of a policy designed to deal with protracted political conflicts. But the terms of debate had already been established, as illustrated in this exchange between political commentator George Will and Indiana Senator Richard Lugar.

> Will: I think when you have nothing but talk, talk is worse than nothing. And it is especially bad when, as in the case of the president's speech the other day, he listed nations involved in state-sponsored terrorism.
>
> Lugar: The fact is, the president spoke before lawyers about law. With strong rhetoric the president laid the groundwork for specific action against perpetrators of the hijacking and also the nation-states that might sponsor it. . . . Our firmness, the fact that we had set the stage and that [the terrorists] could count on retaliation led them to be cooperative in making certain our 39 [hostages] got back to us.
>
> Will: Senator, what I think is a real danger for the president is the worst thing that could happen in politics, and that's laughter. People may begin to laugh at the president when they see that he's indignant, but that he's selectively indignant.
>
> Lugar: George, I find nobody laughing . . . as they contemplate what could have occurred if they had not been cooperative in this instance.
>
> Will: I think we have, therefore, Senator, a point of agreement: That is, that the way to stop the laughter, or to keep it from happening in the first place, is for the rhetoric to be followed by some action. And I gather you're saying it will be.
>
> Lugar: I do say that. I believe the speech was important yesterday in setting the stage and laying the framework for that action. (July 9, 1985)

The expectation and appropriateness of military action were assumed by both speakers, framed in a presentation that simulated the journalistic convention of balance by providing two seemingly opposing viewpoints. The views aired here, however, spoke the language of strength; the discussion revolved around the credibility of "the military option." In addition, the expectation of military action fit the narrative structure of melodrama and closed discussion of alternative approaches to dealing with terrorists.

By the end of 1985, after the hijacking of the *Achille Lauro* ("It's time to take names and kick rear ends," as U.S. Representative Tommy Robinson [D-Ark., 2nd] said, Oct. 10, 1985) and the airport massacres at Rome and Vienna, the United States still retained "its military option" (Dec. 12, 1985) amidst growing public frustration and expectation of action. The credibility of a language of speculation had been exhausted, and network news attention turned to an identifiable target that would enable overt military action.

The Qaddafi Connection

Between January and April of 1986, news narratives about terrorism began to shift from treating terrorism as a general evil to focusing on Libya's Colonel Muammar Qaddafi as the archetypal terrorist. This focus brought into view an identifiable target for retaliation and thus provided a way for the United States to take overt, military action against a symbolic representative of terrorism. Targeting Qaddafi enabled the administration to fulfill foreign policy objectives established early in Reagan's first term. The goal of striking Libya had led to carefully orchestrated disinformation campaigns designed to convince both the news media and the public of the need to punish Qaddafi. For the narrative of terrorism, the Qaddafi connection allowed vindication of the protagonist and temporary closure to the conflict.

Qaddafi had been associated with terrorism long before 1986; on this rationale, the Reagan administration closed the Libyan diplomatic mission in Washington in May 1981. Subsequently, the administration's actions against Libya included an oil embargo, military exercises in the Gulf of Sidra, and the freezing of Libyan assets in U.S. banks. The charges against Qaddafi intensified following the killings at the Rome and Vienna airports. Within days of the massacre, ABC News reported that Italian authorities had established a tentative link that seemed to "point to the shadowy Palestinian terrorist known as Abu Nidal" (Dec. 29, 1985), whose "specialty is the kind of arbitrary act of violence used in the airport attacks: ruthless brutality, calculated to derail any movement towards peace between the Arab nations and Israel" (Dec. 30, 1985). According to ABC News, Qaddafi's support of Nidal implicated him in Nidal's actions and made him "once again the focus of attention for his moral and financial support of terrorism" (Dec. 30, 1985).

Qaddafi's association with a Palestinian is important, because although Qaddafi fits the American ideograph of terrorism by virtue of being an Arab, his lack of direct involvement with Lebanese and Palestinian terrorist groups disassociates him from responsibility for highly publicized terrorist actions such as the bombing of the Marine barracks in Beirut and the hijackings of TWA Flight 847 and the *Achille Lauro*. While Qaddafi was said to have threatened Americans by his responses to perceived U.S. aggression (e.g., Jan. 5, 1986), Nidal presented a more sinister, crazed, and zealous representation of terrorism. He was quoted by ABC reporters as saying that "Reagan is at the top of his hit list," and that if he had "the slightest chance to hurt Americans," he wouldn't "hesitate to do so" (Jan. 8, 1986). At one point Nidal described himself as "more dangerous than an atomic bomb" (Jan. 13, 1986). By reifying a connection between "the Palestinian terrorist leader Abu Nidal and his Libyan patron, Colonel

Muammar Qaddafi" (Dec. 30, 1985), ABC News suggested that Qaddafi was guilty by association, which explained why the Reagan administration continued to "build a case against Abu Nidal and Libya" (Dec. 31, 1985). Within a week, Qaddafi's direct role in the airport massacres was presupposed, as evidenced by White House Press Secretary Larry Speakes' promise: "If Qaddafi *strikes again* and Americans are involved, the United States will be prepared to come down and take drastic action" (Jan. 8, 1986; emphasis added).

Although ABC News mentioned the involvement of Syria and Iran in the terrorist acts for which Qaddafi was blamed, accusations against Qaddafi and speculations of retaliation against him continued throughout January, punctuated by a confrontation between U.S. and Libyan jets in the Gulf of Sidra on the 13th. When a TWA 727 was bombed during a flight from Rome to Athens later that year, network news attention immediately turned to Libya, despite silence from administration officials:

In public, the U.S. government was careful not to point a finger at Libya; in fact, it was not until later in the day that the State Department even acknowledged that the explosion was probably the work of a terrorist. During and after the Gulf of Sidra operation last week, however, there were many threats from Libya's Qaddafi and from Palestinian terrorists Qaddafi supports. (April 2, 1986)

Although administration officials were slow to suggest Libya's involvement, ABC's McWethy expressed confidence in the Libyan connection. This presupposition continued in speculations about military retaliation: "Regardless of who is responsible for today's explosion, officials say the U.S. is not inclined to muscle-flex. The three aircraft carriers that participated in last week's exercise off Libya are all steaming toward port" (April 2, 1986). Military "muscle" was associated with maneuvers off the coast of Libya, thus suggesting that plans for military action were targeted at Qaddafi.

With the bombing of a West Berlin discotheque on April 4, 1986, ABC News fortified charges against Qaddafi in various presuppositions. For instance, the statement, "The terrorist attacks in Greece and West Berlin come a week after U.S. warplanes and ships clashed with Libyan forces in the Gulf of Sidra" (April 5, 1986), implied a causal connection between Libya and the terrorist acts. Presumably, Libya responded to the military exercises with terrorist violence. In saying that "there is no proof *yet* that Qaddafi was behind Wednesday's TWA bombing or yesterday's German nightclub explosion" (April 6, 1986; emphasis added), Donaldson's statement presupposed that such evidence would be forthcoming. U.S. officials continued to "point the finger at Qaddafi," calling him a madman and magnifying his potential for destruction by comparing him with Hitler (April 6, 1986). While before the TWA Flight 840 bombing Qaddafi was described as involved in a complex web of terrorists (Dec. 30, 1985), by April 10, 1986, Qaddafi was described as the mastermind of this web: "The attack on a West Berlin discotheque can be linked to a worldwide network of terrorists *set up by* Colonel Qaddafi" (emphasis added).

Qaddafi's guilt in both the bombing of TWA Flight 840 and the West Berlin nightclub remains to be proven. When the TWA flight was bombed, most sources attributed the act to May Elias Mansur, a Lebanese woman, but Mansur had no proven terrorist connections before the bombing, and evidence was insufficient to result in a warrant for her arrest. And according to West German authorities, the bombing of the discotheque was carried out by Ahmed Nawaf Mansour Hasi, Farouk Salameh, Fayez Sahawneh, and Kristine Endrigkeit under the direction of the Syrian government (Mickolus et al., 1989).

Nonetheless, the establishment of Qaddafi's guilt on television newscasts set the foundation for a highly publicized military strike in retaliation for terrorist acts. On April 9, Donaldson reported that "a strike is in the works," and references to past terrorist acts were dropped as the news reports concentrated on evaluating various military options, including a discussion of which bombers might be best equipped to carry out a strike (April 9, 1986). Finally, ABC News proclaimed that the United States was destined to win the war against terrorism, for "U.S. power is overwhelming" (April 10, 1986). Even when ABC News was "told by high-level Washington sources there will not be an attack on Libya in the near future," reporters stated that U.S. military maneuvers suggested the administration was bluffing, as "the Sixth Fleet is in position to strike at Libya any time the administration decides it might want to" (April 11, 1986). By April 14, ABC announced that "an attack is imminent." At two o'clock the following morning, U.S. F-111, A-6, and A-7 fighter-bombers hit designated targets in Tripoli and Benghazi, damaging civilian and cargo planes, military barracks, the French and Iranian embassies, and Swiss, Finnish, and Austrian ambassadors' residences, and killing two U.S. captains and 36 Libyan civilians.

The U.S. air raid against Libya effectively ended the hero narrative by providing the anticipated overt action taken by the protagonist. Laqueur (1987, p. 286) noted in hindsight that the Libyan connection seemed laughable:

[N]ever before had a person of so little consequence been built up into a demonic figure threatening all mankind [sic], never had a little man who was obviously not quite stable been transformed into a superhuman figure and been taken so seriously. Future historians may find it inexplicable how television turned low comedy into high drama.

In fact, the transformation of Qaddafi into the archetypal terrorist makes sense, given the logic of melodramatic news narratives, which demand overt action taken against a personified villain. Television narratives may be critical in the instant demonization of political adversaries, and the melodramatic imperative of television news makes possible the transformation of minor enemies into villains of mythic proportions.

CONCLUSION

When an act of violence occurs, journalists apprehend the event using a variety of perceptual filters, including semantic and structural frames of terrorism. News coverage of terrorism is characterized by several patterns of presentation with which stories about political conflict are told. The networks' need to sustain audience interest and involvement leads to the use of a standard, melodramatic narrative to frame news events.

Many scholarly descriptions of television news mention the entertainment value sought by news organizations, but few address the specific characterizations of news presentations as they reinforce and validate particular conceptions of foreign policy. Standard dramatic units in ABC News stories about terrorism include the tendency to nominalize visual referents of terrorism, portray government efforts to combat terrorism as ineffective, mobilize viewer emotions through the use of video postcards, and speculate about the effectiveness and probability of military retaliation. News narratives can criticize public officials, thereby reifying an illusory watchdog function while simultaneously suggesting policy options that may support the goals of those officials. Combined, these dramatic units create a narrative exigency for military action taken by the United States against a target that symbolizes terrorism.

Some of our most pressing concerns may be those that address the nature of standardized, commercial news narratives. Television news tells a distinct kind of story, relying on melodrama for narrative structure. Melodrama provides a particular interpretation of events, presenting audiences with clear valences and static actors. Other narrative structures are possible. Tragedy, for instance, can involve the transformation of a hero, society as the source of conflict, and lack of clear resolution. Comedy can provide integration of diversity and reconciliation. In the least, television's reliance on melodrama indicates a lack of creativity in narrative form. And when U.S. journalists tell their stories about terrorism using the conventions of melodrama, replete with paper tigers and video postcards, these news narratives become structurally aligned with an ideology of foreign policy driven by military strength and intervention. Television news coverage of terrorism thus contributes to the building of public support for military intervention rather than for the formulation of policies that can effectively address the causes or prevention of political violence.

6

Official Discourse in the "Age of the Terrorist"

In July 1990, President George Bush dubbed the contemporary period "the age of the terrorist," echoing the theme announced nearly a decade earlier by Ronald Reagan. From international, to "narco-," to "ecoterrorism," the term endures as a focal point of foreign policy. The term "terrorism" is more than a descriptor of political violence; it is also a functional term that warrants certain strategies of response and precludes others. The process by which terrorism gained political currency as the ultimate enemy and the arguments that have followed from this premise illustrate the conjoint construction of ideology in the discourse of news media and high-ranking officials.

Presidents increasingly rely on public evaluations of performance to gain political power, and they concurrently emphasize their role as foreign policy leaders. This role provides them with "substantially more room for maneuver and unilateral action than do the other roles as economic manager or domestic policy initiator" (Marra, Ostrom, & Simon, 1990, p. 251). Specific, unilateral, and dramatic action in foreign affairs enhances the public standing of presidents. As one analysis of presidential popularity demonstrates, "The public has rewarded those presidents who have taken action and have seized the center stage in the theater of foreign policy" (Marra et al., 1990, p. 620). Since people acquire knowledge of presidential action in foreign conflicts primarily through television news (Cohen, Adoni, & Bantz, 1990), presidential popularity depends in part on the degree to which presidents can influence the interpretations made by television news.

Ostensibly, broadcast journalists act as critical watchdogs of foreign policy formation and thus provide an objective vantage point from which government discourse about foreign adversaries can be assessed. Rather than standing apart from the political process of policy formation, however, news media work with and complement particular constructions of the terrorist threat. This focus on political symbols operating within official discourse reveals the degree to which the Reagan administration's construction and use of the term "terrorism" is reflected and legitimated in the language and representations of terrorism presented in televised newscasts.

Many scholars have pointed to the symbiotic relationship between journalists and politicians, noting, for example, the reliance of journalists on official sources for news and visual material and politicians' need for publicity and information. Fewer works, however, address the consensus of images that results from this relationship. Achieving a consensus of images not only depends on the faithful reproduction of official pronouncements; it also requires that media interpretations of political events lie within the same ideological framework as that of official discourse. Ideology is manifest in discursive formations that exist as "an organic and relational whole, embodied in institutions and apparatuses, which weld together an historical bloc around a number of basic articulatory principles" (Laclau & Mouffe, 1985, p. 67). An analysis of the discursive field of terrorism within the Reagan administration reveals the ideological consistency between official and mediated portrayals of terrorism.

In explaining the creation of discursive fields and objects of discourse, Foucault (1977) discusses the ways in which relations of power are coordinated through discursive practices. Such practices are not simply ways of producing discourse; they "are characterized by the delimitation of a field of objects, the definition of a legitimate perspective for the agent of knowledge, and the fixing of norms for the elaboration of concepts and theories" (p. 199). The Reagan administration's process of defining, delimiting, and legitimizing a statist construction of terrorism is evident through analysis of public documents. Because the Department of State, through National Security Decision Directive 30, is responsible for the implementation of U.S. foreign policy and programs dealing with international terrorism, this analysis focused on official statements recorded in the *Department of State Bulletin* and the *Weekly Compilation of Presidential Documents*.

The following analysis traces policy statements about terrorism made by White House and Department of State officials between January 1981 and April 1986. This period includes, but is not limited to, official statements referring to the nine terrorist events covered by ABC News and chosen for this analysis. Although official sources included in ABC newscasts are assessed here, this analysis also encompasses the larger pool of public statements issued by government representatives. Primary attention is given to the discursive practices that gained currency during the Reagan administration and the degree to which these practices reconstructed representations of terrorism on ABC News.

Chapter 3 began by pointing to the frequent dismissal of definitional distinctions between types of political violence and the judgmental nature of calling an act one of "terrorism." ABC News coverage of terrorism was informed by ideographs of terrorism rather than debates over definitions; after five years of terrorism coverage following the Iranian hostage crisis, controversy about definitions finally surfaced. Assumptions similar to those on which the ideograph is based also underlie official definitions and representations of terrorism. For instance, terrorism was depicted as a phenomenon characterized by tactics rather than political goals, and the ideology of the terrorist was explained as fundamentally oppositional to the interests of the United States and the values of democracy.

The depictions and definitions of terrorism presented in official discourse change with the interests of the definers, giving the label of "terrorism" the quality of a persuasive definition. Stevenson (1963) explains: "A 'persuasive' definition is one which gives a new conceptual meaning to a familiar word without substantially changing its emotive meaning, and which is used with the conscious or unconscious purpose of changing, by this means, the direction of people's interests" (p. 32). Definitions of terrorism characteristically included the components of violence and terror. Although the emotive associations with terror remained constant, the political motivations and targets of terrorists shifted with the ideology of the definer. When used as a persuasive definition, terrorism becomes a means of organizing both how we think about terrorism and how we are likely to react to it.

IDEOGRAPHIC RESONANCE IN OFFICIAL DISCOURSE

The concern with definitions usually afflicts academics and political commentators rather than politicians, who are often more concerned with the function of a term than its etymology. Secretary of State George Shultz (1984a) repeatedly expressed his disdain for challenges to official definitions, stating: "The antagonism between democracy and terrorism seems so basic that it is hard to understand why so much intellectual confusion still exists on the subject" (p. 32). He laments (1984b, p. 14):

In recent years, we have heard some ridiculous distortions, even about what the word "terrorism" means. . . . We cannot afford to let an Orwellian corruption of language obscure our understanding of terrorism. We know the difference between terrorists and freedom fighters, and as we look around the world, we have no trouble telling one from the other.

In official discourse, terrorism has been described rather than defined, taking on naturalized qualities conferred by Shultz's authoritative "*we* know" and lending the label characteristics of a persuasive definition.

Maintaining the emotive dimension of the term, official definitions of terrorism stressed the "bestial nature" and cowardice of perpetrators (Shultz, 1983, p. 44). Terrorists were "depraved," showing "psychopathic ruthlessness and brutality" (Shultz, 1984b, p. 14); they were "possessed by a fanatical intensity that individuals of a democratic society can only barely comprehend" (Reagan, 1983a, p. 1746). Reagan (1985a) used this understanding of the terrorist to explain the difficulties of responding to terrorism with military action: "When you think in terms of, for example, immediate force, you have to say 'Wait a minute. The people we're dealing with have no hesitation about murder.' As a matter of fact, most of them even approve of suicide" (p. 808).

Official associations of terrorism with suicide missions and crazed fanaticism simulated presentations of the archetypal terrorist made in ABC News. Concurrent with depictions of the apparent irrationality of the terrorist were references to the criminal nature of terrorism. For instance, Richard Kennedy, undersecretary for management at the Department of State (1981), defined terrorist acts as "illegitimate criminal acts which can be deterred through swift and appropriate judicial action" (p. 66). The coupling of psychotic behavior and criminal action in official definitions ignored a paradox that guides counterterrorism strategies. As Hill (1986) notes, "The U.S. tends to regard terrorists as, at the same time, inhuman fanatics and (implicitly) rational actors who will respond to acts of deterrence" (p. 85).

Consistent with these depictions of terrorists as subhuman, official statements validated conceptions of terrorism as an ahistorical, naturalized phenomenon rather than treating terrorism as a composite term for the violent expression of political grievances. Reagan has called terrorism a cancer, and Shultz (1984b) referred to it as "a contagious disease that will inevitably spread if it goes untreated" (p. 14). Comparisons of terrorism to "natural forces or disasters such as plagues or tidal waves" reinforce the removal of political and social explanation; terrorist acts become "detached from their particular histories and redefined as part of a general phenomenon of our times" (Schlesinger et al., 1983, p. 3).

Decontextualization empties terms of their referential content, leaving openings for new conceptual meanings. In official discourse, terrorism is redefined as containing uniform ideological content identifiable by its opposition to the interests of the United States. Specific ideologies and aims of individual terrorist groups were conflated and homogenized as the Reagan administration subsumed varieties of terrorism under one "overarching goal" of "destroying what we are seeking to build" (Shultz, 1986a, p. 17). Reagan (1983b, p. 61) repeatedly described terrorism as "an attack on all of us—on our way of life and on the values we hold dear," and as opposing "everything we stand for" (1984a, p. 1317).

This oppositional relationship abstracted terrorism so that it functioned as a polar ideograph similar to the frame in ABC News coverage of terrorism. Shultz (1986a, p. 18) clarified the relationship of terms:

Wherever [terrorism] takes place, it is directed in an important sense against *us*, the democracies, against our most basic values and often our fundamental strategic interests. The values upon which democracy is based—individual rights, equality under the law, freedom of thought and expression, and freedom of religion—all stand in the way of those who seek to impose their ideologies or their religious beliefs by force. A terrorist has no patience and no respect for the orderly processes of democratic society and, therefore, he considers himself its enemy.

Terrorists became, by definition and thus by political motivation, the enemy of U.S. democracy. This emphasis on U.S. democracy is important because it illustrates one of the many distortions in official definitions of terrorism. In official discourse, terrorism was organized in opposition to the principles of democracy. Yet in practice, not all democracies are terrorized; for instance, such attacks are rare in Scandinavian countries (Morgan, 1989).

In the passage above, Shultz also shifted responsibility for designation of the label to the terrorist, as if the United States were merely responding to a self-proclamation of enemy status made by terrorists. This shift abdicated the United States from responsibility for creating the conditions to which the terrorist responds. Popular portrayals of terrorists legitimize the official version, so that when terrorists cite previous actions taken by the United States as justification for their actions, these rationales are usually absent from official and network versions of the incident. The unidirectional presentation of self-described terrorists acting in an historical void was illustrated during the TWA Flight 847 hijacking, during which the hijackers shouted, "Marines," and "New Jersey," and asked if the passengers remembered the Bir al Abed massacre, in which Lebanese CIA operatives killed more than 80 civilians. The confused passengers could not understand these angry references to past U.S. actions in Lebanon (Mayer & McManus, 1988). This definitional redirection posed the United States as an innocent victim and allowed the administration to treat terrorists semantically as criminals and strategically as enemies, thus denying the terrorists political status while at the same time justifying retaliatory tactics reserved for such actors.

This polarization of terrorism and democracy in official discourse allowed the user of terms flexibility in attaching labels to political actors. The directions in which this definition of terrorism was taken in official discourse will be explored throughout this chapter. Before continuing, however, a point of contrast must be made, for although the persuasive definition constructed in official discourse dominated many discussions of terrorism, it was, of course, only one of many perspectives toward terrorism. Dominant definitions of terrorism and the representations they validate are instructive both for what they include as objects of discourse and for what they exclude. Alternative constructions of terrorism can be found in "counterdefiners," whose voice is muted in mainstream news media and nonexistent in the official lexicon of persuasive definitions. A brief survey of counterdefinitions of terrorism provides a contrast to and perspective on the degree to which official depictions of terrorism resonated with the ideographic constructions of television news.

COUNTERDEFINITIONS OF TERRORISM

Implicit in official discussions of terrorism is the assumption that terrorism is practiced solely by non-state actors. Terrorism is the tactic of the powerless and the uncivilized. Conceived in this manner, terrorism is never conducted by incumbent governments; neither can these governments be implicated in the creation of the conditions that give rise to terrorism. Paradoxically, the targets of state-sponsored "counterterrorism" rarely consist of a few crazed nihilists acting without a popular constituency. Rather, they consist of viable political adversaries who threaten the stability of an international order defined as legitimate by the United States and its allies.

One of the most developed critiques of official definitions of terrorism has come from Herman and Chomsky, who have focused on the hypocrisy of excluding discussion of state terror as supported by the United States in Third World countries such as El Salvador, Guatemala, and Nicaragua from definitions and discussions of terrorism. In El Salvador and Guatemala, U.S. support of repressive regimes has led to terror unacknowledged in official discourse and media accounts:

During the years 1980–84 the death squads worked freely in El Salvador, in close coordination with the army and security forces. The average rate of killings of civilians in the thirty months prior to the 1982 election was approximately seven hundred per month. Many of these victims were raped, tortured, and mutilated. All of this was done with complete impunity, and only the murder of four American women elicited—by dint of congressional pressure—any kind of legal action. . . . In Guatemala, too, the endemic fear based on years of unconstrained and continuing army violence was a dominant fact of national life. (Herman & Chomsky, 1988, p. 105)

In establishing a functioning terrorist state in El Salvador (Chomsky, 1988a) and supporting the state-organized violence of Guatemala, the United States has been participating in what Herman calls wholesale, or state terror (1982).

Wholesale terror takes two forms. First, as in the examples of El Salvador and Nicaragua, wholesale terror exists when governments terrorize their own citizens. This kind of terrorism is difficult to comprehend, because the state is typically the only institution allowed to use force and violence legitimately. Conceptions of state violence as terrorism thus meet considerable resistance in official circles. Duvall and Stohl (1988) raise this conceptual problem to preface their distinction between forms of state violence, calling state terrorism a subset of official repression. In advancing a theory of governance by terror, they refine conceptions of wholesale terror and challenge official characterizations of terrorism, such as the requisite that terrorists seek publicity.

According to Herman and Chomsky, government support for terrorist acts carried out by groups inside another country constitutes the second form of wholesale terror. This type of terrorism is exemplified in U.S. support for the contras: "In the case of Nicaragua, we repeat the central fact that differentiates it from the U.S. client states: in 1984 its government was not murdering civilians. The main fear of ordinary citizens in Nicaragua was of violence by the contras and the United States" (Herman & Chomsky, 1988, p. 106).

Although official discourse also includes terrorism practiced by states or their agents, actions taken by the United States or its allies are generally outside the scope of discussion. Thus, while terrorism in Nicaragua may be addressed in official discourse, it appears within the framework of the ideograph. The Rand Corporation's summary of international terrorism in Nicaragua reflects this approach, as the only acts of international violence acknowledged in its survey of terrorism during 1982–83 consist of Nicaraguans hijacking planes in attempts to leave the country (Cordes et al., 1984). While support for terrorist activity from an outside government constitutes international terrorism, Nicaraguans using force to flee their own country does not constitute an international act.

Similar criticisms regarding official versions of state sponsorship of terrorism have been leveled against the United States' treatment of terrorism in the Middle East. Chomsky (1988b; 1990) has challenged U.S. and Israeli policy toward Palestinians and Lebanese. Citing Israel's campaign of "terror against terror," Chomsky notes the U.S. government and media's labeling of raids on Tunis and Beirut as "retaliation" rather than terrorism. Government officials recognize this difficulty in acknowledging state actions as constituting terrorism and admit that "counting direct actions as terrorism would make it difficult not to count some of Israel's activities" (Lardner, 1991, p. 38). The problem of including state action in discussions of terrorism is counterproductive for any incumbent government, as discussions of state terrorism might cast doubt on the legitimacy of that government's own use of force and violence.

Finally, counterdefiners often challenge official definitions of "retail" terrorism, distinguished from state terror as the terror of isolated individuals and small groups (Herman, 1982). Retail terror is the form most often occupying official discourse. As Perdue (1989) states, "Guerilla tactics of the powerless are more apt to be labeled terrorist than martial force on the part of an established state" (p. 3). Emphasis on retail terrorism serves many functions for institutional definers; Herman (1982) claims that "retail terrorism is overblown for political reasons, to distract attention from more substantial terror, and to allow a manipulation of public fears and a more efficient 'engineering of consent' " (p. 212).

Although this brief summary of counterdefinitions does not provide an expose of the "more substantial terror" to which Herman refers, attention to alternative depictions of terrorism as presented by counterdefiners illuminates the boundaries erected by official definitions of terrorism. Works such as those cited above point to gaps in the discursive formation and ways to challenge the selective picture of international terrorism drawn by government officials. Additionally, counterdefinitions serve as a reminder of the degree to which terms are constructed to serve the interests of institutional definers.

DRAMATIC FACTS

Just as official discourse presents definitions of terrorism as unambiguous and self-evident, it also presents the factual world of terrorism as certain and unproblematic. Statistics give force to ideographs and become, as Gusfield (1981) has called them, dramatic facts. As knowledge about a public problem is gathered, "it is fashioned into a public system of certain and consistent knowledge in ways which heighten its believability and its dramatic impact" (Gusfield, 1981, p. 53). Through the use of statistics, both journalists and politicians added legitimacy to the significance of terrorism as an object of discourse and as constituting a threat of crisis proportions. Although ample evidence indicated no substantial increase in terrorism since 1980 (Celmer, 1987; Kupperman, 1986; Roberts, 1986; Stohl, 1988;

Targ, 1988), reports produced by administration officials showed dramatic increases in terrorist activity, especially in acts against U.S. citizens and property. Concurrently, network news reports featured statistics compatible with the inflated versions provided in official discourse.

As presented in Chapter 2, the construction of dramatic facts in ABC News coverage of terrorism began as early as March 1981, less than two months after Reagan's inauguration, with ABC's feature of a CIA report on the recent increase in terrorism. As news coverage escalated over the next five years, documentation about the terrorist threat proliferated in both newscasts and official discourse. In 1982, a Department of State report gave information ignored in later versions of the terrorist threat: "Both the number of international incidents and the number of casualties resulting from incidents fell in 1981. Deaths caused by terrorist attacks dropped dramatically from 642 in 1980 to 173 in 1981." The geographic area in which terrorism "has been increasing faster than in other parts of the world" was Latin America, where "more attacks were recorded in 1980–81 than in any other two-year period since 1968" ("Patterns of International Terrorism," 1982, pp. 9–15). Even without the inclusion of state-sponsored terrorism in its compilation of statistics for Latin America, the emphasis on terrorism in that region and on an overall decline in deaths caused by international terrorism challenged the subsequent public statements of escalation made by politicians and journalists.

Public pronouncements and reports on terrorism gradually increased in 1982 and 1983. At the end of 1983, Reagan (1983a) announced that terrorism had "multiplied" by "three or four times as many incidents" since 1968, and "53 percent of those have been aimed at American—at United States targets" (p. 1747). Several problems are inherent in Reagan's statistics. Perez (1982), writing in the *Department of State Bulletin*, stated that in 1980, U.S. citizens and "U.S. interests" represented 38 percent of terrorist targets. Subsequent Department of State reports provided similar figures; in 1981, U.S. citizens were targets of "more than 40%" of all terrorist acts ("Patterns of International Terrorism," 1982), and Dam (1984), the acting secretary of state, reported a 40 percent figure for 1983. Reports produced both within and outside of the administration placed the percentage of U.S. targets at approximately 40. Reagan's statistic of 53 percent more closely resembled the percentage of diplomats who were the targets of terrorist acts; according to the Department of State, in 1980, attacks on diplomats constituted 54 percent of all terrorist attacks (Perez, 1982), and in 1983, diplomats were the target in 52 percent of the terrorist incidents (Sayre, 1984). But even these statistics refer to diplomats in general, rather than U.S. diplomats.

Further problems existed in determining what to include as an international terrorist incident and how to establish the target of an attack. Wilkinson (1986) notes some of the inconsistencies in counting acts of terrorism that produce considerable variation in even the best-known data bases on international terrorism. The discrepancies are due not only to differences in definitions of terrorism but also in categorization of what constituted an "incident." For example, the Rand Corporation's chronology of international terrorism "treated a wave of 40 bombings as a single incident, whereas the CIA's data base dealt with it as 40 separate incidents" (p. 45).

In addition to differences in defining "terrorism" and "incident," statistics were also compiled using a range of measures for "international" and "target." Wilkinson (1986) continued: "The geographical location of incidents is fairly reliably recorded, even allowing for differences in definition. But there is no comprehensive cross-national data-base on the nationality of targets, only a selection of national sources" (p. 46). Given the U.S. government's primary reliance on news reports and intelligence gathering that are relevant to U.S. interests as a data base, official statistics disproportionately emphasized the degree to which U.S. interests were threatened. Although this exaggeration of threat might have prompted increased caution on the part of potential victims, this emphasis on U.S. liability also legitimates the ideographic construction of terrorism as inherently oppositional to Western interests and the use of extreme measures to counter the threat.

Compounding the problem of compiling statistics, administration officials often used "target" and "victim" interchangeably (e.g., Reagan, 1984a), despite the fact that Americans could suffer from terrorist incidents as victims without having the attack directed at them. Finally, the use of "interests" is problematic. "Interests" cannot be terrorized, and official statistics often conflate attacks against citizens with those targeting property or military personnel.

This latter distinction is particularly important regarding statistics for 1983. In his April 26, 1984, message to Congress, Reagan stated (1984b, p. 591):

In 1983 more than 250 American citizens were killed in terrorist attacks, the largest number in any year of record. . . . In the past fifteen years, terrorism has become a frightening challenge to the tranquility and political stability of our friends and allies.

The years "of record" to which Reagan referred began in 1968, the point at which the U.S. government began compiling statistics on terrorism and, not coincidentally, the time at which Reagan recognized an emergent challenge posed by terrorism. More significant, however, was Reagan's inclusion of casualties in the October 1983 bombing of the Marine barracks in Beirut. Although the Marines were eulogized as having been killed during their performance of a military mission (conducted during conditions of civil war in Lebanon), they were defined by the State Department as "noncombatants" and are thus included in counts of civilian casualties. If military personnel were excluded from official statistical inventories, the recorded numbers of U.S. deaths from terrorism would be substantially smaller. Morgan (1989) refigured the statistics this way, finding that "in no one year of the 1980s was the number of U.S. civilian fatalities due to terrorism higher than thirty" (p. 30).

Just as counterdefinitions do not serve the interests of administration officials, low statistics do not provide evidence of a crisis. They are not dramatic. Regardless of whether the statistical manipulations found in official discourse were designed to magnify the threat of terrorism, official versions of the problem had the net effect of dramatization. This official discourse was legitimized by ABC News accounts, which increased the dramatic value of the statistics. During coverage of each terrorist event, ABC News grounded the perception of crisis in dramatic facts. On June 24, 1985, ABC News reported a "30 percent increase in international terrorism in the last year," a misleading figure, given the drop in terrorist incidents in 1983. Although terrorist acts did increase in 1984, they merely returned to 1982 levels (Kupperman, 1986). In addition, Department of State estimates of the level of terrorist violence in 1984, on which news reports were likely to have been based, underwent "statistical refinements." For instance, "terrorist acts by rural insurgent groups in Asia, Africa, and Latin America, which were not counted in previous years, were included in 1984. This was, of course, bound to inflate the figures" (Laqueur, 1987, p. 312).

Department of State statistics also varied depending on the claims they were used to support. In the June 1985 *Department of State Bulletin*, Oakley, the director of the Office for Counter-Terrorism and Emergency Planning, reported that during 1984, the "total number of international terrorist incidents" had risen "some 30%—a total of over 650 compared to 500, the figure for 1983 and the average of the previous five years" (1985a, p. 73). But in the November 1985 *Department of State Bulletin*, Oakley cited more than *600* terrorist incidents in 1984, which accounted for "a *20%* increase over the average level of the previous 5 years" (1985b, p. 62; emphasis added). The discrepancy can be explained by Oakley's comparison of terrorist acts during 1985 and 1984. Because he included only part of each year in his comparison, the statistics were skewed. Oakley stated: "The number of incidents is up further this year—480 for the first 8 months, compared with 382 for the same period last year" (1985b, p. 62). This increase was less than that between 1983 and 1984, and suggested a slowing of the escalation of terrorism.

Statistics that showed a slowing in the escalation of terrorism served two functions. The threat posed by terrorism remained credible, as the percentage increase was still high enough to cause concern. But by the end of 1985, public pressure to take dramatic action against terrorists was mounting, and the administration needed to demonstrate some measure of control over the problem and some success of U.S. counterterrorism measures. By December 1985, Charles Redman, a spokesman for the Department of State, appeared on ABC News with a further downward revision of the statistic, claiming that terrorist attacks were growing "at a rate of about 15 percent a year" (Dec. 27, 1985). Consistent with the goal of the administration, Peter Jennings explained this lower figure as the result of State Department counterterrorism efforts.

Statistics used by ABC News in coverage of terrorism consistently dramatized the impact of terrorism as well as its frequency. For instance, ABC News emphasized the effectiveness of terrorist attacks by reporting that "over 90 percent of all terrorist acts have been successful." To define success, Jennings explained, "If someone wanted to explode a bomb, they are successful, at least initially" (June 26, 1985). Of course, proving that a terrorist wanted to explode a bomb but did not do so is difficult at best; by Jennings' definition, the performance of almost any terrorist act was successful due to the occurrence of the act itself.

Although some discrepancies existed in ABC News statistics about terrorism, facts were generally used to show an ever-increasing threat posed by terrorists. Over an 18-day period at the end of 1985, Jennings reported that according to Department of State records, there were "630 separate terrorist attacks" in 1985 (Dec. 27, 1985). Four days later, correspondent Richard Threlkeld reported: "The State Department said today that between January and November this year, 695 terrorist incidents were carried out" (Dec. 31, 1985). These facts became more dramatic as ABC News coverage continued. On January 13, 1986, Jennings told viewers:

In an almost daily barrage of reports on terrorism, you certainly get a sense of how significant a problem this has become. Some information from our Fact File: Two years ago, there were approximately ten incidents of terrorism, by U.S. definition, every week. Today, there are ten every day.

Department of State documents do not verify this 700 percent increase in terrorist activity.

This last observation should not be taken to imply that Jennings was fabricating information about terrorism. Rather, his dramatic facts were probably provided by an administration official or institutional expert equally interested in demonstrating the dramatic significance of terrorism. A survey of all sources receiving air time during ABC News coverage of the terrorist events included in this analysis reveals ABC's reliance on Department of State officials. Using the categories developed by Hallin, Manoff, and Weddle (1989), all 283 sources receiving air time were coded for their institutional affiliation (or lack of one). During ABC's coverage of terrorism, current and former U.S. government officials accounted for 52.7 percent of testimony aired; 17.7 percent of the statements were provided by foreign officials; 18 percent came from non-government "experts"; 5.6 percent consisted of remarks made by non-government foreigners. The remaining 6 percent of the statements were defined as "other" (e.g., law enforcement officials, media representatives, political commentators). Corporate representatives were present in the sample; advocacy groups were not. The ABC News emphasis on Department of State officials is clear; statements from officials in the executive branch constitute 69 percent of those made by government officials.

In their study of newsgathering practices among print and television journalists, Ericson, Baranek, and Chan (1987, p. 292) explain the consequences of the journalist's dependency on established sources:

[I]t is sufficient for the reporter to quote source A making truth claim "X" . . . rather than independently seeking and establishing his own version of the truth. Indeed, probing efforts that result in discovery of competing facts can soften the hard facts of source quotations, and even lead to a version of the truth of the matter that results in having no story to report. . . . Reporters are therefore inclined to go no farther than the performative utterance of official sources.

This reliance on official sources results in the reproduction of dramatic facts that reinforce and legitimize the construction of terrorism presented by administration officials.

Given the variety of statistics available about incidents of terrorism, media representations of official discourse constitute a site at which institutional perspectives and crisis designations can be legitimated. The relative drama of data on terrorism reflects the interests of the presenter. Facts about terrorism vary due to selective perception and decontextualization of political violence, and statistical measures necessarily reflect the perspective of the researcher (Laqueur, 1987). The dramatic facts presented in official discourse and televised news coverage of terrorism provide an illusion of certainty in situations in which publics have a heightened need for information and must rely on media representations of reality. Finally, although the escalation of fear encouraged by dramatic facts may indirectly aid the terrorist, a more direct and cooperative relationship exists between network news divisions and government officials arising from the networks' need to create drama and the goal of the Reagan administration to place counterterrorism high on the public agenda.

CREATING AND COMBATING CONSPIRACY

The Reagan administration's degree of control over definitions of and facts regarding terrorism granted considerable power to these custodians of official discourse. The ideological content of terrorism as antithetical to democracy operates at an abstract level. In a move that maximizes the utility of the term, the administration associated terrorism with the specific actors deemed adversaries by the U.S. government. The use of the terrorist label to delegitimize perceived enemies is not new; for instance, U.S. descriptions of Southeast Asia in the 1960s included references to the Viet Cong's "terror tactics." But the elevation of terrorism to an ideograph, aided by television news accounts, added considerably to the political currency of the term. The process of designating adversaries as terrorists occurred in two stages of official discourse. First, definitions of and facts pertaining to terrorism were increasingly linked to sovereign states to justify Reagan's (1985b) construction of "Murder, Incorporated," a worldwide conspiracy of terrorist states; second, military retaliation as a viable counterterrorism measure was increasingly advanced as the appropriate response to the actions of the newly identified terrorist nations. This latter set of policy objectives, forwarded by Secretary of State George Shultz, has been called the "Shultz Doctrine" (Celmer, 1987).

Both strategies must be understood in the context of the Reagan administration's early attempts to implicate the Soviet Union in acts of international terrorism. Shortly after Reagan's inauguration, Secretary of State Alexander Haig affirmed the Soviet Union's connection to terrorism in his first press conference: "When you get to the bottom line, it is the Soviet Union which bears a major responsibility today for the proliferation and the hemorrhaging of international terrorism as we've come to know it" (In Cline & Alexander, 1984, p. 21). Haig (1981, p. 9) continued this theme throughout 1981:

I have been one who has pointed out that when the Soviet Union funds, supports, conducts training courses in the Soviet Union and its Eastern European satellites, when it aligns itself with the provision of arms and perhaps more to such state-supported terrorist activities as those of Qadhafi in Libya or Castro in Cuba, that they must bear a measure of responsibility for these activities.

These charges and others like them were dutifully reproduced in the mainstream press, accompanied by editorials and magazine cover stories that claimed links between the Soviet Union and Japanese, West German, and Italian terrorist groups (Parenti, 1986).

This tying of the war on terrorism to the war on communism was not unique to the Reagan administration. For instance, in 1974, the threat of domestic terrorism was linked to "foreign communist terrorists." In 1975, proceedings from the Senate Internal Security and Senate Committee of the Judiciary hearings reported: "It has been established that the Communists, despite their repeated declarations that they do not engage in terrorist activities, do in fact provide training and logistical support for terrorist groups" (in Perdue, 1989, p. 11). But following the allegations made early in Reagan's first term, official discourse and media reports targeting the Soviet Union subsided. In the news media, the " 'Soviet terrorism' theme receded from the news as quickly as it had appeared, with no explanation as to why the public was no longer being alerted to this menace and no demand from the press for an explanation" (Parenti, 1986, p. 150). Official proclamations of the Soviet connection dissipated during 1982, resurfacing in the form of "Murder, Incorporated" in 1984 and 1985.

Charges of Soviet-directed terrorism subsided after 1981 largely because of the lack of evidence to sustain them. Shortly after Haig's January 1981 press conference came the publication of Claire Sterling's book, *The Terror Network*, which used case studies of the IRA in Northern Ireland, Turkish terrorists, and the Italian Red Brigades to conclude that the Soviet Union was sponsoring and directing a worldwide terror network. Not only did this book receive substantial attention in the prestige press (Herman, 1982; Parenti, 1986), but the galleys for the book informed Haig's understanding of the Soviet role in international terrorism (Woodward, 1987). Subsequent coverage of Sterling in *The New York Times Magazine*, beginning with Haig's assertion of Soviet involvement, led CIA Director William Casey in search of support for Sterling's thesis.

Evidence of Soviet involvement could not be found. Not only were Sterling's methods denounced by CIA staff members, but independent CIA-sponsored investigations could not substantiate Sterling's conclusions or Haig's public statements. By May 27, 1981, a secret CIA report stated that the Soviet Union was not "the hidden hand behind international terrorism" and illuminated ironies such as Sterling's reliance on information "from an Italian press story on the Red Brigade. The story was part of an old, small-scale CIA covert propaganda operation" (Woodward 1987, pp. 127–129). These findings and the discrediting of Sterling's thesis were not publicized.

Outside of government circles, academics such as Herman (1982) developed detailed criticisms of Sterling's work. And three years after publication of *The Terror Network*, the *Washington Post* ran a series of articles "which concluded that there could be found no 'significant information of Soviet involvement in terrorist enterprises' " (Parenti, 1986, p. 150). By this time, however, the target of official discourse had shifted such that evidence of direct Soviet involvement was no longer necessary to legitimate the severity of the threat posed by international terrorism.

"Murder, Incorporated"

Equating terrorism with the Soviet Union limited the scope of the term and the ideology of the terrorist to one of communism. By the mid-1980s, a more developed construction of terrorism circulated in official discourse, one that relegated the Soviets to a more ambiguous role and that could implicate a broader range of adversaries under the label of terrorist. Policy statements regarding terrorism rose slowly in 1981 and 1982 and were covered dutifully by the news media. Media reports escalated rapidly in 1983 and 1984, concurrent with the increase in policy pronouncements and debates. Official discourse and media reports both helped to construct a consensus of images about the nature of the terrorist threat and the appropriateness of responses to it that validated Reagan's foreign policy objectives. One function of this consensus is that it unites audiences against perceived injustices. But "from the standpoint of the state," this unity can also be used to "magnify the threat and to weave a pattern of conspiratorial power in order to make a credible foe" (Perdue, 1989, p. 9). This conspiracy was dubbed by Reagan (1985b) as "a new, international version of 'Murder, Incorporated.' "

The identification of specific states as supporters of terrorism existed before Reagan's formulation of "Murder, Incorporated"; for instance, Syria, Cuba, and Libya were frequently identified as sponsors of terrorism (Kennedy, 1981; Kampelman, 1981; Perez, 1982). But these states were presented as having ties to the Soviet Union, thus still implicating that country. Cassese (1989, p. 16) explains the U.S. position:

[T]he other superpower foments or directs terrorists by remote control, or it sends its "cutthroat retainers" to do so. Hence every terrorist movement is connected to a sovereign state (Libya, Syria, Iran, etc.) which in turn is operating on behalf of a greater power in the other camp.

After the 1983 bombings of the U.S. Embassy and Marine barracks in Beirut, Soviet involvement was downplayed to the level of support and encouragement rather than direction, and responsibility was placed more squarely with states such as "Iran, the regime of fanatics with which we have had earlier experience" (Shultz, 1983, p. 44).

By 1984, the credibility of the crisis status given to terrorism was bolstered by the association of terrorist acts with state adversaries. Reagan stated in an April

1984 message to Congress: " 'State' terrorism, starkly manifest in the recent dreadful spectacles of violence in Beirut, Rangoon, and Kuwait, accounts for the great majority of terrorist murders and assassinations" (1984b, p. 591). As Perdue (1989) recognizes, the "delegitimizing label of terrorism has been reserved" for "significant adversaries" (p. 8). In 1985, Reagan (1985b, p. 8) targeted these adversaries in a speech before the American Bar Association:

So, there we have it: Iran, Libya, North Korea, Cuba, Nicaragua—continents away, tens of thousands of miles apart, but the same goals and objectives. I submit to you that the growth in terrorism in recent years results from the increasing involvement of those states in terrorism in every region of the world. This is terrorism that is part of a pattern, the work of a confederation of terrorist states. . . . [A]ll of these states are united by one, simple criminal phenomenon—their fanatical hatred of the United States, our people, our way of life, and our international stature.

Reagan did make some attempt to link these states together by their association with communism; for instance, he noted that "only recently the Prime Minister of Iran visited Nicaragua bearing expressions of solidarity from the Ayatollah for the Sandinista communists." But above all, these five states were joined in their "real goal" to "expel America from the world" (Reagan, 1985b, p. 8).

The motivation of terrorist groups had been defined as one of destroying "our country's most basic interests, policies, and values" (Reagan, 1984c, p. 247), and the naming of these nations as terrorist seemed natural within official discourse. Naturalization also occurred in ABC News coverage of the speech. Donaldson reported (July 8, 1985):

Mr. Reagan all but declared war on five nations, which he said are terrorist havens. (Edited video from Reagan's speech: "Core group of radical and totalitarian governments, a new international version of Murder, Incorporated. We must act together, or unilaterally if necessary, to ensure that terrorists have no sanctuary anywhere.") The president claimed the right of self-defense under international law against five states: Iran, Libya, Cuba, North Korea, and Nicaragua. The State Department terrorism list, published only last week, omits North Korea and Nicaragua and names South Yemen and Syria instead. So thanks to the role played by Syrian President Assad in ending the hostage crisis, Syria's apparently undergoing at least temporary rehabilitation.

The justification and appropriateness of devising such a list went unquestioned, as it fell within the ideological framework of official discourse. The next day, noting that President Reagan had "called some people a lot of names," Jennings asked political commentator George Will and Senator Richard Lugar, "Does it help his cause, or does it hurt?" The only objection to Reagan's list came from Will, who criticized Reagan for excluding Syria and the Soviet Union (July 6, 1985). Will and Lugar focused on the need to respond to terrorism with military action, a discussion that assumed the legitimacy of "Murder, Incorporated" and fit neatly in the parameters of responses to the problem of terrorism as established by the Shultz Doctrine.

The Shultz Doctrine

On April 3, 1984, Reagan signed National Security Decision Directive 138, which endorsed in principle the use of preemptive strikes and military raids against terrorists, called for greater use of covert actions and counterintelligence operations, and established military and CIA hit teams designed to strike at terrorists and their bases (Celmer, 1987). The same day, Shultz delivered an address before the Trilateral Commission in which he articulated the Shultz Doctrine, or the "use of force in implementing U.S. foreign policy and in combatting terrorism in particular" (Celmer, 1987, p. 63).

The Shultz Doctrine was more than an extension of Reagan's call for "swift and effective retribution" for terrorists; it also introduced legal rationalization for military actions and attempted to extend presidential power. Shultz (1984b, p. 14) repeated the official ideology of counterterrorism and argued that the threat of terrorism constituted a perpetual state of war:

In the 1980s and beyond, most likely we will never see a state of total war or a state of total peace. . . . As the threat mounts—and as the involvement of such countries as Iran, Syria, Libya, and North Korea has become more and more evident—then it is more and more appropriate that the nations of the West face up to the need for active defense against terrorism.

"Active defense" included preemptive military strikes and retaliation based on rules of war rather than those of criminal justice. Shultz (1984c) stated that in this "disorderly and dangerous new world," where terrorism is "a weapon of unconventional war against democratic societies," the United States must not "opt out of every contest" but rather use "our power for good and worthy ends." And "anyone who believes that military support for our friends isn't crucial to a just outcome is living in a dream world" (pp. 13–14).

Shultz (1984b, p. 16) escalated the intensity of his appeals six months later in an address before the Park Avenue Synagogue in New York city:

We now recognize that terrorism is being used by our adversaries as a modern tool of warfare. It is no aberration. We can expect more terrorism directed at our strategic interests around the world in the years ahead. To combat it, we must be willing to use military force.

Shultz spoke the official language of the terrorism ideograph to justify the use of force, calling terrorists "depraved opponents of civilization itself," with "freedom and democracy" as their targets (1984b, p. 13). He dismissed U.S. actions abroad from any role in contributing to conditions inciting terrorism: "We are attacked not because of some mistake we are making but because of who we are and what we believe in" (1984b, p. 15).

Finally, Shultz called on public support for increased "flexibility to respond to terrorist attacks in a variety of ways" (1984b, p. 16). According to the Shultz Doctrine, flexibility had been hampered by "a web of restrictions on executive action embedded permanently in our laws" and by "constraints on timely action" due to congressional involvement in the formation of foreign policy. Shultz explained: "Micromanagement by a committee of 535 independent-minded individuals is a grossly inefficient and ineffective way to run any important enterprise" (1984c, p. 15).

Shultz realized that foreign policy based on presidential prerogative must have public support. His policy of combatting terrorism with overt military force required

a broad public consensus on the moral and strategic necessity of action. We will need the capability to act on a moment's notice. There will not be time for a renewed national debate after every terrorist attack. We may never have the kind of evidence that can stand up in an American court of law. But we cannot allow ourselves to become the Hamlet of nations, worrying endlessly over whether and how to respond. (Shultz, 1984b, pp. 16–17)

The creation of public support for military responses to terrorism necessitated by the Shultz Doctrine was aided by both increased news coverage of terrorism and Reagan's rhetoric of response. Shultz's calls for military action came before the sensational terrorist acts of 1985—the hijacking of TWA Flight 847, the murder of Leon Klinghoffer aboard the *Achille Lauro*, and the massacres at the Rome and Vienna airports—and thus set, in advance, the discursive formations within which official counterterrorism policies would be discussed.

The Shultz Doctrine did not go unchallenged in official circles; among the strongest opponents to Shultz was the Secretary of Defense, Caspar Weinberger (Bell, 1989). But Weinberger eventually supported the Shultz Doctrine, perhaps due to his desire to strike Qaddafi. Reagan's CIA had described Qaddafi as the "most prominent state sponsor of and participant in international terrorism since 1981" (Dobson & Payne, 1982, p. 56), and the United States had subsequently tried to provoke Qaddafi into a military confrontation as a pretense to use force against him (Hersh, 1987). As illustrated earlier, the administration was sorely in need of a military target to confer credibility to repeated threats of retaliation against terrorists. The "flamboyance of Kaddafi's personality and attitudes made him a natural target or whipping boy, a proxy for governments more crucial but more discreet or less vulnerable, like Syria or Iran" (Bell, 1989, p. 81). Identification of Qaddafi as the archetypal terrorist thus benefitted both the news media by providing dramatic value and the administration by providing a "safe"—and strategically desirable—target.

Shultz's position was thus undoubtedly aided by televised news coverage of terrorism, which helped create audience expectations of military action. By the time of the 1986 U.S. air strike against Libya, Weinberger had called terrorism " 'a method of waging war' planned, organized and financed by governments," thereby invoking the right of self-defense as justification for military reprisals (Bell, 1989).

Official discourse characterized by assumptions such as those in the Shultz Doctrine might have been particularly well suited to reproduction in television news. Wardlaw (1988) discusses news coverage of terrorism as mobilizing the kind of public panic used to justify policies such as those advocated by Shultz and carried out under Reagan. He notes (1988, p. 217) that

governments have often been the willing accomplices of the news media in generating and maintaining the hysteria which surrounds terrorism and have thus themselves been guilty of subverting the process of accurate threat assessment. The result has been that the issue of international terrorism has assumed monumental proportions.

Of course, if the larger aim of an administration is to use the perception of threat to justify a particular ideology of foreign policy, then accurate threat assessment might hamper the progress toward broader goals. The elevation of international terrorism to a problem of crisis proportions, the consolidation of power advocated by Shultz, and the increasing legitimacy of military responses to terrorism all dominated official discourse and created a consensus of images about terrorism that was compatible with media representations of the terrorist threat.

CONCLUSION

Analysis of official discourse reveals the degree to which White House and State Department constructions of terrorism reinforce and are reconstructed in representations of terrorism provided by ABC News. Persuasive definitions and dramatic facts both legitimized terrorism as an ideograph and lent credibility to the designation of terrorism as constituting a crisis. Additionally, the nature and escalation of the threat as presented in official discourse justified the naming of adversaries as terrorists and supported increasingly repressive policies toward terrorism.

ABC News coverage of terrorism complemented official discourse in a variety of ways and helped build public support for foreign policy modeled after the Shultz Doctrine. Shultz (1985b, p. 79) seemed to recognize the implications:

I regard the general movement of opinion about terrorism and the importance of it, and the importance of doing something about it, as very healthy. We've been trying to wake people up, and I think they're thoroughly awake and that's good, because that means as things take place they'll be broadly supported.

Ironically, Shultz summarized the successful creation of a semantic crisis, one in which public anxiety is engendered and used to rationalize policies that require sacrifice or repression (Edelman, 1977).

The implications of this crisis extend beyond past responses to terrorism. First, defining terrorism as an act of war against democracy "effectively ends debate about whether military responses are justified: If a country is at war, it must respond militarily to an attack" (Simon, 1987, p. 112). This ideological closure emulates what was created by the narrative of terrorism provided by ABC News coverage (see Chapter 4). Further, since jurisdiction of the problem fell within the Department of State, strategies for fighting this war are formulated within the official domain by which diplomacy, not war, is conducted. The functions of the Department of State and Department of Defense have been blurred, and the doctrine of diplomacy through force may have been normalized.

At a tactical level, the construction of the crisis in terrorism bolstered the emerging U.S. policy of military intervention in low-intensity conflict (LIC):

L.I.C. doctrine, taken as a whole, develops a paranoid conception of geopolitical relations, portraying a grandiose West under attack from persecutory and conspiratorial elements. In this context, the full range of Western institutional and operational violence is defined as self-defense. (Perdue, 1989, p. 199)

The thematic structure of LIC doctrine is well suited to the ideological framework provided by official and media constructions of terrorism. Perdue uses a U.S. Army Command and General Staff College report (1983) to summarize key features of the doctrine, which include: an understanding of national liberation movements as "instrumental, tactical, and ahistorical"; an assumption of U.S. interests as "good for the Third World"; a conspiratorial theme that includes both the Soviet Union and "the entire Arab bloc of nations"; a concern with image enhancement through media support; and a major role for "special forces" in counterterrorism. Strategies of intervention in LIC include the use of "war games" to "send signals" and the development and support of Special Operations Forces such as the Delta Force, Navy SEALS, and Rangers (Perdue, 1989, pp. 198–200). These strategies play well in news programs that portray foreign policy in symbolic gestures and espouse technological and military responses to complex problems.

Finally, terrorism in official discourse conveniently represents a malleable label, its referential meaning shifting with the political goals of primary definers, the group "best able to ideologically structure the process of signification such that its own interests are served" (Mumby, 1989, p. 303). As "a form of warfare waged by political forces—including some sovereign states—that are hostile to democracy and determined to undermine the position of the West" (Shultz, 1986b, p. 41), terrorism functions as a more inclusive term than communism. Hitchens (1986) remarks: "The word 'terrorist' is not—like 'communist' or 'fascist'—being abused; it is itself an abuse. It disguises reality and impoverishes language and makes a banality out of the discussion of war" (p. 68). While the dominant construction of terrorism provides a more open range of targets for the U.S. government, it simultaneously limits the range of U.S. responses to terrorism to ones of retaliation and repression.

7

Conclusions: Political Violence in a Video Age

Since the 1986 retaliatory air raid against Libya, international terrorism has shown no signs of abating. Terrorists continue to plant bombs, hijack planes, and threaten civilian populations with random violence. Government officials continue to use the label of terrorist to define political adversaries as the embodiment of evil. And television news continues to tell stories about terrorism based on a narrative logic that privileges foreign policy based on military strength.

Fortunately, few U.S. citizens have been the victims of international terrorism. Rather than gaining an understanding of terrorism through personal experience, Americans are likely to learn of terrorism through news media. Television news gives audiences a highly stylized picture of terrorism. It provides stories about terrorism that are molded by the expectations of audiences, the preconceptions of journalists, and the materials of violence and political discourse that surround such events. The features of news narratives about terrorism are noteworthy not just for the public reality of terrorism that they come to define but also for the larger relationship between news and foreign policy that they reveal. Understanding ABC News' coverage of terrorism is one step in the process of comprehending the larger ideological system to which television contributes.

Accounts of terrorism in ABC *World News Tonight* constructed terrorism as a public crisis deserving immediate attention and government response. The absence of imminent danger that international terrorists posed to most Americans and the lack of consensus about the significance of the terrorist threat rendered this crisis a semantically created one. In other words, terrorism had been depicted in a manner that engendered widespread anxiety and panic and that could be used as a political tool to further policies designed to respond to it. The crisis designation imposed by journalists constitutes a way of thinking about events; for journalists, it is a means of discovering and understanding news.

Several presentational elements characterized the reality of the crisis constructed by journalists on ABC News. Terrorism was presented as an ahistorical, depoliticized phenomenon exemplified by the archetypal Islamic fanatic. Elevated to the status of ideograph, terrorism served as a semantic frame by which events were understood. Although the concept of "frame" has received much attention and is used frequently in analyses of media, scholars apply the construct inconsistently, at times referring to the process of news selection and values and at other times describing a form of visual and verbal presentation. This analysis suggests that a conceptual distinction can be made between the two types of frames. Frames occur at two levels, one of orientation and another of story. Each level reconstructs and informs the other. First, ideographs provide semantic frames that often constitute a journalist's common sense. They provide an orientation for apprehending events and a culturally based myth that guides news narratives, and they establish precedent in the knowledge of journalists.

Semantic frames in news reports are socially determined. Journalists draw from the meanings and values circulating in their social and political environment. But since journalists are concerned primarily with the knowledge and opinions of the political and authoritative sources with whom they are in regular contact, semantic frames of terrorism are determined largely by those officials who claim ownership of the problem about which the journalist reports. Journalists thus participate in the reproduction of dominant ideology at the stage of apprehending events as well as describing them.

The second kind of frame is a structural one. Structural frames provide the story forms that television journalists use to tell audiences about terrorism. The narrative form used in television news coverage of conflict structures events using the qualities of melodrama. The clear moral valences required in melodrama readily evolve from the opposition inherent in ideographs and serve as a vehicle of social unification against perceived evil. News stories thus have the capacity to mold moral orders and claim credibility through the narrative form on which they rely. Audiences expect the teller of the tale, the anchor, to preside over events, they expect the interests and motives of political actors to be identified, and they expect some measure of resolution at the conclusion of the narrative. In contemporary media, audience expectations are built and then satisfied through dramatic narratives that simplify moral ambiguity and resolve conflict with the actions of a protagonist.

The use of melodramatic frames as the forms by which news stories are told had observable consequences in television coverage of terrorism. ABC News reports of terrorism, framed as melodrama, resulted in a narrative that nominalized visual referents of terrorism, portrayed official protagonists as incompetent, mobilized viewer emotions of terror and frustration, and posed the need for dramatic military action. The melodramatic imperative structurally aligned ABC News' narratives with an ideology of foreign policy driven by principles of military strength and intervention.

Approaching news as narrative constitutes one of the ways by which conventions of journalistic objectivity can be questioned. Other conventional features of news presentations allowed journalistic interpretation to be overlooked. Interpretation of events appeared under the guises of decontextualization, background reports as special assignment series, and the language of speculation to create scenarios about future events. Decontextualization situated events in the present, removing them from material conditions and reframing them according to narrative conventions. Where a news context was unfamiliar to viewers, special assignment series provided the conventions by which particular incidents were understood. Finally, through the language of speculation, reporters described events that *might* happen and relied on statements of probability to justify the relevance of their interpretations. In ABC News coverage of terrorism, the language of speculation legitimized the crisis designation for terrorist events as reporters constructed scenarios of future dangers and crises.

LIMITATIONS

Before extending the implications this analysis suggests, it would be prudent to note the limitations inherent in this study. The research process is never complete; of course, the relationship between constructions of terrorism in television news and those in official discourse deserves further exploration. At the outset, an additional relationship needs to be understood: although this analysis assumes audience involvement in the presentations of terrorism offered by ABC News, it cannot account for the individual and varied interpretations that might be made by audience members. Audience perceptions of terrorism and foreign conflict may be less constrained by popular media genres other than television news. For instance, Elliott, Murdock and Schlesinger (1986) argue that British feature films present portrayals of terrorism which are open to more diverse interpretations among audience members. This argument deserves to be tested, as a cursory glance at made-for-TV movies such as *Voyage of Terror: The Achille Lauro Affair*, or feature films like *Die Hard*, suggests that popular U.S. media may be remarkably consistent (and static) in their portrayals of terrorism. Diversity in portrayals might exist in alternative non-fiction programming; Viera (1988) claims that the self-referential style of some documentaries can address the limitations in journalistic conventions of reporting about terrorism. Variations may be discovered, but U.S. media are resilient in perpetuating traditional stereotypes about Arabs, including the myths that all Palestinians are terrorists and that Arabs are "fabulously wealthy," "barbaric and uncultured," and "revel in acts of terrorism" (Shaheen, 1984). Even with the apparent pervasiveness of these myths, accounts of public perceptions of terrorism would be enhanced by attention to media portrayals of terrorists that circulate outside the domain of television news and by complementing textual analysis with audience studies.

Additional limitations were created by the focus on one news organization and its coverage of major acts of international terrorism. Comparisons of ABC *World News Tonight* with CBS *Evening News* and NBC *Nightly News* might be instructive; however, most research suggests that television news portrayals of terrorism are similar. For instance, in their analysis of network coverage of three terrorist groups, Paletz, Ayanian, and Fozzard (1982) reported: "The three networks' coverage of the three groups was extremely similar. They reported the same events, and depicted them similarly. Violence and governmental response were emphasized; terrorists' goals, objectives, perspectives were neglected" (p. 157). More recent studies also find consistency in the network news formats used to cover terrorism (Atwater, 1989). Given this apparent homogeneity, comparisons of the three networks to alternative news programs or formats might be more instructive.

The scope of this analysis was also limited by the focus on major news stories. This sample resulted in stories that concentrated on terrorism in the Middle East and thus inadvertently reflected the same disproportionate emphasis on Middle Eastern terrorism as that provided by ABC News. Although inclusion of a broader range of stories might have altered the general character of news depictions of terrorists, significant differences seem unlikely due to the dominant media emphasis on Middle Eastern terrorism. For instance, in surveying nine weeks of ABC, CBS, and NBC weekday evening newscasts, Wittebols (1990) found that 78 percent of the stories using " 'terror' words" were related to official enemies in the Middle East such as Palestinians, Libyans, and Iranians. Middle Eastern terrorism clearly provides the backdrop for television portrayals of terrorists; further research could investigate the degree to which the patterns of depiction that have been apparent in news coverage of extended and highly publicized terrorist incidents are reproduced in coverage of terrorism in other regions such as Central America and Asia.

Finally, the approach used here sacrificed attention to the location of individual stories within the rest of the newscast and to detailed analysis of the relationship between verbal and visual depiction. Analysis of story placement is in many respects a different project than the one undertaken here. However, attention to the location of individual news accounts about terrorism and transitional devices surrounding news stories may yield added insight about the ways in which public problems are imbued with crisis dimensions. In news coverage of terrorism, perceptions of magnitude may be enhanced by linking devices such as "story clusters," or adjacent stories that are linked thematically to terrorism. Paletz, Ayanian, and Fozzard (1982) write in their comparison of network coverage of the IRA, Red Brigades, and FALN (Puerto Rican Armed Forces of National Liberation): "Such connections can influence, even determine, viewers' perceptions of an event. Approximately 11 percent of the terrorism stories were adjacent to stories about other terrorist violence" (p. 150). In the ABC News accounts investigated here, stories about Middle Eastern terrorism were clustered with those about terrorism in El Salvador, and special assignment reports linked coverage of terrorism to stories about counterterrorism in private industries and about the fears Iowa farmers had of neo-Nazi extremists. Further investigations of these linkages between stories and their relative placement in newscasts may reveal a broader process of depiction, whereby journalists create news landscapes from the smaller portraits they have drawn.

Additional attention can also be given to the relationship between verbal and visual depiction in network newscasts. People may read and speak with a verbal language, but the medium of television privileges learning through images. The emphasis here was placed on visual nominalizations as reinforcing ideographic interpretations of terrorism, and the methodology used implicitly privileged verbal depiction with visual material treated as a supplement to verbal narrative. This approach approximated Robinson's (1984) description of verbal text as "a metadiscourse for the visual"; sound "allows for the semantic fixing or binding of images by the spoken text in television news. This accords with Raymond Williams's idea that television is, above all else, the maintenance of a *flow*. This continuity is possible only through the predominance of verbal links" (p. 202). Journalists tell viewers how to understand visuals, and they provide thematic transitions between sequences of images. These words can contradict the visuals, though, and some images may create strong perceptions regardless of the words used to explain them. In television coverage of terrorism, the images used to depict events are often more powerful than the disclaimers surrounding them. Thus, images may contribute to an interpretation of events that an individual journalist wishes to discredit.

The force of visuals used in coverage of terrorism, particularly the ample depictions of military prowess, has been given extensive attention here. The potential for contradictions between visual and verbal components of news narratives about terrorism may be relatively limited, because coverage is usually based on reconstructions of video images rather than live narration of events. News producers thus have greater control in choosing actuality footage that reinforces the prevailing interpretation of the event. However, inconsistencies can arise; visuals may overpower or contradict the narration provided by journalists, rendering the relationship between modes of presentation one that deserves further exploration.

IMPLICATIONS: NEWS AND FOREIGN POLICY

The visual nature of television news poses unique problems for our understanding of foreign conflict. Television establishes the frames within which stories will be told. Those frames will focus on visual events and dramatic conflict, and they will be placed in a narrative structure that commands the broadest public appeal. Our perceptions of terrorist acts are shaped by the manner in which we come to understand them, and the particular way in which we understand conflicts influences our reactions to them. Television news thus helps to set the terms by which foreign policy is understood, and those terms will fit a visual, melodramatic narrative. The implications are considerable, not just for our knowledge of terrorism, but also for our development of foreign policy.

The Narrative Logic of Television News

Media critics have long lamented television's tendency to decontextualize, fragment, and sensationalize news. Ideological critiques point to the networks' reliance on institutional sources and the media's general adherence to the government's point of view (as long as it is compatible with advertisers). But the narrative logic of contemporary television news makes its own contribution to public understanding of crisis and may require us to rethink the relationship between television and democracy.

In television news, description often substitutes for explanation. What we often overlook is that description implies an attitude, a point of view. Television relies on stereotypes for the sake of simplicity or ease of depiction, providing us with, for instance, portrayals of Arabs as crazy, suicidal, religious fanatics. These stereotypes spill over from the terrorists, informing our judgments about all Arabs, and turning pictures of people into an explanation for what is happening. This conveniently fits the logic of the narrative, in which Americans are innocent victims of incomprehensible actions and U.S. policy is in no way implicated in the chaos of the Middle East.

The visual authority and melodramatic logic of television add to the relative ease with which enemies can be transformed into mythic demons. Imagery and allegory are the forms by which demons are constructed, and television narratives excel in their use of both. Television lends a new degree of credibility to official allegations about the terrorist status of designated opponents. Prior to the U.S. invasion of Panama, Manuel Noriega instantly became a narco-terrorist, and during the Persian Gulf war, Saddam Hussein was condemned for committing incomprehensible, irrational acts of eco-terrorism despite the fact that, weeks earlier, the Department of State had said that his taking of Western hostages had not constituted terrorism. In both cases, use of the terrorist designation was timed for its political expedience and used to mobilize the collective commitment of the U.S. public to the use of military intervention. And in both cases, television news located these figures within a symbolic narrative that lent credibility to the designation.

Collective commitment is also mobilized through instant characterizations appearing in the form of video postcards, a particular kind of news story emanating from coverage of TWA Flight 847. As defined here, a video postcard is a personal message sent by a victim or hostage to friends or family members. In essence, a person uses television news to talk to someone he or she cannot reach. Video postcards are now a conventional part of television news; during the Persian Gulf war, the video postcard took the form of "postcards from the desert," or messages between troop members and their families. This kind of private communication presented on public broadcasts helps viewers experience frustration and fear, serving the dual function of involving viewers emotionally in the newscast and presenting the news media as a concerned institution that gives people a chance to communicate with one another. The continual agony of affected families combined with government inaction results in excruciating public frustration, and, in some cases, humiliation. If this emotional engagement is combined with dramatic action, the narrative is successful because it ends in the manner that audiences expect and desire. Video postcards thus put the administration in a prime position to achieve public consensus over foreign policy, as long as the policy fits the narrative logic of swift and decisive action.

This is precisely the option most often presented on television news. Military retaliation becomes the most talked about and seemingly most viable way to deal with terrorists and, perhaps, other political adversaries. Television allows reporters to speculate, to build visual scenarios about what might happen. These speculations establish the seriousness of threats and the measures that are desirable to take. This is not the same as deliberation about options, as scenarios suggest that the option depicted is the one most likely to be taken. Scenarios are also difficult to challenge, for although journalists may comment on visual presentations, there are rarely countersimulations that present possibilities other than those suggested by the incumbent administration. Without visuals to verify the commentary, the credibility of the scenario is less compelling. In times of peace, television news draws from Department of Defense file footage, coverage of military exercises, computer simulations, and action-adventure movies such as *Top Gun*. In times of war, and with careful planning and control by the military, television news can move beyond speculation.

Television news does far more than focus our attention on an event. The ways that stories are told have important implications for our understanding of foreign conflict and the kinds of policies we are likely to support. The information we get is guided by principles such as the dramatization of facts, hero plots, video postcards, and emphasis on immediate, visible action. The narrative logic of television news gives us a plot structure that doesn't necessarily fit the natural occurrence of events but gives us a story that takes us through all of the emotional stages of a good drama. This puts us in a position to react to events rather than question or understand them.

Keeping Clean: The Function of Television Commentary

Television news might be structurally aligned with certain types of foreign policy, but the first concern of news organizations is furthering their own legitimacy rather than the legitimacy of a government. News organizations need to deflect criticism in a manner that maintains or enhances their credibility. In the case of terrorism, television news frequently has been blamed for its escalation of terrorism, and criticism has often been made in the terms established by the contagion theory: Does news coverage aid the terrorist? News organizations must address this issue; "someone has to be mortified/victimized to expiate the guilt created by the violation of conflicting commandments, the humiliation, and the fear and sense of vulnerability created by terrorists." According to Dowling (1989), "television prefers to mortify itself" (p. 11). Mortification serves the function of purification, for in grappling with this question, news organizations purify their role by reasserting their aura of objectivity and their value as a public messenger.

Extended coverage of foreign crises often results in numerous television news reports and special programs designed to raise and respond to criticisms regarding press performance. In these reports, news organizations defend their actions by appealing to the public service they had provided or to the lack of control journalists have over the structure and content of news stories. A special assignment report aired on July 3, 1985, illustrated this process. Correspondent Sander Vanocur opened the segment: "Terrorism. From beginning to end, the drama of TWA 847 resembled a made-for-television movie. It had heroes, emotion, killers, joy, death, and sorrow. But ultimately, it had a happy ending."

Vanocur presented the melodramatic narrative as intrinsic to the hijacking; these dramatic units, however, were a perspective from which the news media viewed events rather than inherent features of a social act. Vanocur continued, noting that critics had charged that "it was a crisis which television had exploited. In effect, that television was hijacked by the terrorists" and had provided "a worldwide platform to the terrorists."

Certainly, there are limitations of this understanding of the relationship between media and terrorism, as was argued extensively in Chapter 2. But instead of dealing with these problems, ABC redirected the issue to one of public service rather than aiding the terrorists. ABC News legitimated and popularized its coverage by showing public reliance on the "video connection" between hostages and their families that had been provided by the ABC newscasts. Vanocur reviewed these functions of ABC's reports and concluded: "By a two-to-one margin, the public approves of the way networks covered the crisis" (July 3, 1985). Public opinion polls became (and, it seems, still are) the grand arbiter of challenges to news format and content.

Self-criticism of journalistic performance that ends in self-congratulation helps justify the role of news coverage of terrorism and enhances the credibility of the news media as providing a mirror on the world. ABC's credibility was further bolstered by acting as a forum for mediation and a source of information for government officials during ongoing terrorist events. Given the no-concessions policy of the United States, public statements reproduced in the news media have become a primary method of discussion and negotiation between governments, terrorists, and their supporters (Kupperman, 1986). During its self-critique, ABC News indirectly praised itself for providing a forum for negotiation. As one "conflict resolution expert" testified during an ABC special assignment report: "Much of what the media did was very constructive. It helped the Americans understand the problem in human terms." ABC's correspondent Bill Blakemore followed this comment with the elaboration that journalists play the role of third-party negotiators by "opening lines of communication," "clarifying the real underlying issues," and "exploring for possible solutions" (July 4, 1985). This self-congratulatory position taken by ABC News fit well with the administration's emphasis on public affairs; ABC's role ensured coverage of public statements made by government officials who use news media to communicate with other nations.

Image-Driven Policy

As television increasingly mediates foreign conflict, the role of journalists in crafting political discourse becomes pivotal in the process of orchestrating public opinion about crises and formulating policies to respond to them. Television functions politically, structuring reality for both the viewing public and political leaders. Even presidents watch television for information about unfolding events, occasionally making major foreign policy decisions based on news coverage (Kupperman & Kamen, 1989). But television journalists, even inadvertently, do not lead the policymaking process. Rather, contemporary television news complements a political process that is reliant on public images for legitimacy and guidance. Increasingly, presidents have turned to news media for publicity, culminating in Reagan's "public relations style" of media management. Presidents also recognize that dramatic political action in foreign affairs can translate to power and popularity at home. Terrorist incidents provide opportunities for public statements and symbolic gestures, but administrations that are reliant on media strategies of photo opportunities and image enhancement are also prime targets for terrorists. As Bell (1989) explains: "If you deal largely in images and 'photo opportunities' as a foreign-policy technique, few things provide more touching images or better photo opportunities than grateful released hostages and happily weeping wives shaking hands with the President" (p. 82). Paradoxically, although hostage-taking can constitute short-term public dramas with ample photo opportunities, basing diplomatic style on image enhancement and preoccupation with terrorism also suits the objectives of the terrorists.

The need to sustain popularity through public images also obliges politicians to reproduce constructions of terrorism circulated by the news media. In a sense, when policymakers tailor policy with media images in mind, media images can drive policy. And because the nature of televised news imparts specific qualities to images, media presentations are suited to particular kinds of policy, ones based on grand symbolic gestures, overt demonstrations of force, technological prowess, and lack of historical contextualization. Network news coverage of terrorism in the 1980s illustrates the conjoint construction of conflict through news representations and official discourse that validate one another, and it exemplifies the process by which images and ideologies are normalized in a system of discursive practices.

FROM CRISIS TO CHAOS: THE POLITICS OF PERPETUAL WAR

Americans continue to worry about the threat of terrorism. In 1986, U.S. citizens listed terrorism as their primary concern, ranking ahead of the economy, environmental pollution, drugs, poverty, homelessness, and external national attack (Morgan, 1989). The concern remains, as Americans cite terrorism as a justification for warfare and cancel flights abroad because of it. The danger is real, but it comes as much from our own role in escalating and perpetuating violence as it does from the random acts of insurgent terrorists.

Rather than directly aiding the terrorist, news coverage of terrorism reproduces an ideology of counterterrorism that justifies an approach to international conflict guided by symbolic gestures and overt military force. Presenting terrorism as a morality play fits both the narrative structure of television and the doctrine of low-intensity conflict. News media are thus structurally aligned with official discourse. This structural alignment is based partly on the global interests of the media, but the relationship is more incestuous than purely economic models suggest. And although some scholarly descriptions of network news mention the entertainment imperative of television news organizations, few address the specific characteristics of news presentations as they reinforce and validate particular conceptions of public policy. This analysis demonstrates ways in which television news is implicated in a broader ideological system that legitimizes particular constructions of terrorism.

The constructions of terrorism identified here perpetuate specific principles by which foreign policy is formulated. First, counterterrorism is normalized; repressive measures justified to combat terrorism in the face of a crisis can be carried on as normal practice due to the shifting definition of terrorism. When terrorism is constructed as an ideograph that by definition stands in opposition to U.S. interests, options for the use of military force become legitimate in any situation that is deemed "anti-democratic" by the White House. The emotive content of the term "terrorist" provides a ready-made moral panic that can be attached to various adversaries and used to justify special military operations. In this manner, producers of the dominant ideology control signification and thus perceptions of conflict. If, as Mumby (1989) writes, "ideology mobilizes meaning in a particular way—it creates a certain relationship between sign and referent which predisposes social actors toward a certain interpretation of an event" (p. 297), then journalists are coproducers of a text that supports counterterrorism.

One application of the shifting relationship between sign and referent has emerged with official use of the term "narco-terrorist." Clyde Taylor, deputy assistant to the secretary for International Narcotics Matters, has acknowledged that legally, "terrorism cannot be used to describe narcotics traffickers and their organizations" (1985, p. 85). However, Taylor and other administration officials have proceeded to make this connection, explaining that terrorism is financed by narcotics traffickers "who are governed only by their greed and whose ideology—if it can be called one—is the pursuit of profit" (Taylor, 1985, p. 85). This ideology is arguably that of most U.S. corporations, but this irony escapes unnoticed within the boundaries of official discourse. Constructions of the "narco-terrorist" are instrumental in the war on drugs, justifying policies ranging from military intervention abroad to increased funding for domestic surveillance programs. G. William Harwood, manager of government programs for Flir Systems, producers of infrared detection devices, noted that the fight against "narco-terrorists" has kept alive many special Department of Defense programs in an era of relaxed tension between the United States and the Soviet Union.

Normalization of counterterrorism thus serves many policy objectives, from elevating the status of political adversaries to expanding the budgets of special operations forces. Perpetual panic over terrorism also distracts attention from contradictions and voids in U.S. foreign policy. Some critics have recognized that "counterterrorist rhetoric has been geared largely toward converting public anxiety over political violence into support for militarist foreign policy and increased intervention in the Third World" (Lee, 1989, p. 18). Constructions of terrorism in network news and official discourse contribute to the building of support for policies that serve the goals of military intervention rather than the formulation of policies that can effectively address the causes or prevention of terrorism.

The construction of terrorism as a public crisis also indicates deeper chaos created by U.S. attempts to exert influence in an era of perpetual war, in which empires are extended through covert actions and fighting by proxy. The contemporary era is characterized by shifting alliances among nations and the dislocation of state sovereignty with geographic boundaries. Under these conditions, official constructions of terrorism may forestall the knowledge necessary to deal with "increasing fragmentation, a diffusion of power, and a sustained challenge to the sovereign state's once natural monopoly of force" (Der Derian, 1989, p. 234). While serving political needs at home and justifying repressive policies abroad, dominant U.S. constructions of terrorism inhibit the process of international cooperation needed to address the challenges posed by political violence. And by reinforcing and legitimizing official constructions of terrorism, television news contributes to the cycle of responses that may ultimately serve the cause of the terrorist.

Bibliography

Adams, W. C. (1985, August). The Beirut hostages: ABC and CBS seize an opportunity. *Public Opinion*, 45–48.

Adams, W. C. (1978). Network news research in perspective: A bibliographic essay. In W.C. Adams & F.C. Schreibman (eds.), *Television network news* (pp. 11–46). Washington, DC: George Washington University.

Adler, R. P. (ed.), (1981). *Understanding television*. New York: Praeger.

Alexander, Y. (1979). Terrorism, the media, and the police. In R. Kupperman & D. Trent (eds.), *Terrorism: Threat, reality, response* (pp. 331–348). Stanford: Hoover University Press.

Alexander, Y., & Finger, S. (eds.), (1977). *Terrorism: Interdisciplinary perspectives*. New York: John Jay Press.

Alexander, Y., & O'Day, A. (eds.), (1984). *Terrorism in Ireland*. New York: St. Martin's Press.

Alger, D. E. (1989). *The media and politics*. Englewood Cliffs, NJ: Prentice-Hall.

Altheide, D. L. (1991). The impact of television formats on social policy. *Journal of Broadcasting and Electronic Media, 35*, 3–21.

Altheide, D. L. (1987). Format and symbols in TV coverage of terrorism in the United States and Great Britain. *International Studies Quarterly, 31*, 161–176.

Altheide, D. L. (1987). Formats for crises. *Phi Kappa Phi*, Fall, 12–14.

Altheide, D. L. (1984). Media hegemony: A failure of perspective. *Public Opinion Quarterly, 48*, 476–490.

Altheide, D. L. (1982). Three-in-one news: Network coverage of Iran. *Journalism Quarterly, 59*, 482–486.

Altheide, D. L. (1981). Iran vs. U.S. TV news: The hostage story out of context. In W. C. Adams (ed.), *Television coverage of the Middle East* (pp. 128–157). Norwood, NJ: Ablex.

Altheide, D. L. (1976). *Creating reality*. Beverly Hills, CA: Sage.

Anzovin, S. (ed.), (1986). *Terrorism*. New York: H.W. Wilson.

Atwater, T. (1989). News format in network evening news coverage of the TWA hijacking. *Journal of Broadcasting & Electronic Media, 33*, 293–304.

Bassiouni, M. C. (1982). Media coverage of terrorism: The law and the public. *Journal of Communication, 32*(2), 128–143.

Bell, C. (1989). *The Reagan paradox: U.S. foreign policy in the 1980s*. New Brunswick, NJ: Rutgers University Press.

Bennett, W. L., & Edelman, M. (1985). Toward a new political narrative. *Journal of Communication, 35*(4), 156–171.

Benson, T. W. (1983). Implicit communication theory in campaign coverage. In W. C. Adams, (ed.), *Television coverage of the 1980 presidential campaign* (pp. 103–113). Norwood, NJ: Ablex.

Bird, E. S., & Dardenne, R. W. (1988). Myth, chronicle, and story: Exploring the narrative qualities of news. In J. W. Carey (ed.), *Media, myths, and narratives: Television and the press* (pp. 67–86). Newbury Park, CA: Sage.

Bremmer, P. L. (1987, March). Practical measures for dealing with terrorism. *Department of State Bulletin*, pp. 1–4.

Brown, W. J. (1990). The persuasive appeal of mediated terrorism: The case of the TWA flight 847 hijacking. *Western Journal of Speech Communication, 54*, 219–236.

Brown, W. J. (1987, May). *Mediated communication flows during a terrorist event: The TWA flight 847 hijacking*. Paper presented at the International Communication Association Conference, Montreal.

Bruck, P. A. (1989). Strategies for peace, strategies for news research. *Journal of Communication, 39*(1), 108–129.

Buhle, P. (1987). *Marxism in the United States*. New York: Verso.

Burke, K. (1984). *Attitudes toward history*. Berkeley: University of California Press.

Carey, J. W. (1986). Why and how? The dark continent of American journalism. In R. K. Manoff & M. Schudson (eds.), *Reading the news* (pp. 146–196). New York: Pantheon.

Carpini, M. X., & Williams, B. A. (1984). Terrorism and the media: Patterns of occurrence and presentation. In H. Han (ed.), *Terrorism, political violence and world order* (pp. 103–134). Lanham, MD: University Press of America.

Cassese, A. (1989). *Terrorism, politics, and law: The Achille Lauro affair*. Princeton, NJ: Princeton University Press.

Celmer, M. A. (1987). *Terrorism, U.S. strategy, and Reagan policies*. Westport, CT: Greenwood Press.

Chatman, S. (1990). *Coming to terms: The rhetoric of narrative in fiction and film*. Ithaca: Cornell University Press.

Chatman, S. (1978). *Story and discourse: Narrative structure in fiction and film*. Ithaca: Cornell University Press.

Chomsky, N. (1990). *Pirates and emperors: International terrorism in the real world*. Brattleboro, VT: Amana Books.

Chomsky, N. (1988a). *The culture of terrorism*. Boston: South End Press.

Chomsky, N. (1988b). Middle East terrorism and the American ideological system. In E. Said & C. Hitchens (eds.), *Blaming the victims* (pp. 97–148). London: Verso.

Cline, R. S., & Alexander, Y. (1984). *Terrorism: The Soviet connection*. New York: Crane, Russak, & Co.

Clutterbuck, R. (1975). *Living with terrorism*. London: Faber and Faber.

Cohen, A. A., Adoni, H., & Bantz, C. R. (1990). *Social conflict and television news*. Newbury Park, CA: Sage.

Cohen, S., & Young, J. (eds.), (1981). *The manufacture of news: Deviance, social problems, and the mass media*. Beverly Hills, CA: Sage.

Comstock, G., & Cobbey, R. E. (1978). Watching the watchdogs: Trends and problems in monitoring network news. In W. C. Adams & F. Schreibman (eds.), *Television network news* (pp. 47–64). Washington, DC: George Washington University.

Condit, C. M. (1987). TV articulates abortion in America: Competition and the production of a cultural repertoire. *Journal of Communication Inquiry, 11*(2), 47–59.

Connolly, W. E. (1984). The politics of discourse. In M. Shapiro (ed.), *Language and politics* (pp. 139–167). New York: New York University Press.

Cordes, B., Hoffman, B., Jenkins, B. M., Kellen, K., Moran, S., & Sater, W. (1984). *Trends in international terrorism, 1982 and 1983*. Santa Monica, CA: Rand Corporation (Publication no. R-3183-SL).

Cornfield, M. (1988). The Watergate audience: Parsing the powers of the press. In J. Carey (ed.), *Media, myths, and narratives: Television and the press* (pp. 180–204). Newbury Park, CA: Sage.

Dam, K. W. (1984, December). Terrorism in the Middle East. *Department of State Bulletin*, pp. 73–74.

Davies, H., & Walton, P. (1983). Death of a premier: Consensus and closure in international news. In H. Davies & P. Walton (eds.), *Language, image, media* (pp. 8–49). Oxford, England: Basil Blackwell.

Davis, D. K. (1990). News and politics. In D. L. Swanson & D. D. Nimmo, *New directions in political communication: A resource book* (pp. 147–184). Newbury Park, CA: Sage.

DeFleur, M. L. (1982). *Theories of mass communication*. New York: Longman.

Der Derian, J. (1989). The importance of shredding in earnest: Reading the national security culture and terrorism. In I. H. Angus & S. Jhally (eds.), *Cultural politics in contemporary America* (pp. 230–239). New York: Routledge.

Diamond, E. (1982). *Sign off*. Cambridge, MA: MIT Press.

Dobkin, B. A. (1989). Rhetorical depiction of terrorism as an instrument of U.S. foreign policy. *Speech Communication Annual, 3*, 121–135.

Dobson, C., & Payne, R. (1982). *Counterattack: The West's battle against the terrorists*. New York: Facts on File.

Dowling, R. E. (1989, February). *The media and the terrorist: Not innocents, but both victims*. Paper presented at the Western Speech Communication Association Conference, Spokane, Washington.

Dowling, R. E. (1986). Terrorism and the media: A rhetorical genre. *Journal of Communication, 36*(1), 12–24.

Dreyfus, H. L., & Rabinow, P. (1983). *Michel Foucault: Beyond structuralism and hermeneutics* (2nd edn.). Chicago: University of Chicago Press.

Duvall, R. D., & Stohl, M. (1988). Governance by terror. In M. Stohl (ed.), *The politics of terrorism* (pp. 231–272). New York: Marcel Decker.

Edelman, M. (1988). *Constructing the political spectacle*. Chicago: University of Chicago Press.

Edelman, M. (1977). *Political language*. New York: Academic Press.

Edelman, M. (1976). *The symbolic uses of politics*. Urbana: University of Illinois Press.

Elliott, D. (1988). Family ties: A case study of coverage of families and friends during the hijacking of TWA flight 847. *Political Communication and Persuasion, 5*, 67–75.

Elliott, P., Murdock, G., & Schlesinger, P. (1986). "Terrorism" and the state: A case study of the discourses of television. In R. Collins, J. Curran, N. Garnham, P. Scannell, P. Schlesinger, & C. Sparks (eds.), *Media, culture, and society* (pp. 264–286). London: Sage.

Epstein, E. C. (1977). The uses of "terrorism": A study in media bias. *Stanford Journal of International Studies, 7*, 67–78.

Epstein, E. J. (1973). *News from nowhere*. New York: Vintage.

Ericson, R. V., Baranek, P. M., & Chan, J. B. (1987). *Visualizing deviance*. Toronto: University of Toronto Press.

Esslin, M. (1982). *The age of television*. San Francisco: W. H. Freeman.

Ettema, J., & Glasser, T. (1988). Narrative form and moral force: The realization of innocence and guilt through investigative journalism. *Journal of Communication, 38*(3), 8–26.

Falk, R. (1986, June). Thinking about terrorism. *The Nation*, 873.

Fishman, M. (1982). Crime waves as ideology. In S. Cohen & J. Young (eds.), *The manufacture of news: Deviance, social problems, and the mass media* (pp. 98–117). Beverly Hills, CA: Sage.

Fiske, J. (1987). *Television culture*. London: Methuen.

Foss, S. J. (1989). *Rhetorical criticism: Exploration & practice*. Prospect Heights, IL: Waveland Press.

Foucault, M. (1977). *Language, counter-memory, practice*, D.F. Bouchard (ed.). Ithaca, NY: Cornell University Press.

Fuller, L. K. (1988). Terrorism as treated by *The Christian Science Monitor, 1977–1987*. *Political Communication and Persuasion, 5*, 121–137.

Gal-Or, N. (1985). *International cooperation to suppress terrorism*. New York: St. Martin's Press.

Gans, H. J. (1979). *Deciding what's news*. New York: Vintage Books.

Genovese, M. (1988). Terrorism. In R. E. Hiebert & C. Russ (eds.), *Impact of mass media* (pp. 143–154). White Plains, NY: Longman.

Gerbner, G. (1988). *Symbolic function of violence and terror*. Unpublished manuscript. Boston: Emerson College, Terrorism and the News Media Research Project.

Gerbner, G. (1973). Cultural indicators: The third voice. In G. Gerbner, L. P. Gross, & W. H. Melody (eds.), *Communications technology and social policy: Understanding the cultural revolution* (pp. 555–573). New York: John Wiley & Sons.

Gewen, B. (1987, September 7). Taking on terrorism. *The New Leader*, pp. 17–18.

Gitlin, T. (1980). *The whole world is watching*. Berkeley, CA: Free Press.

Goffman, E. (1974). *Frame analysis: An essay on the organization of experience*. New York: Harper and Row.

Good, L. (1989). Power, hegemony, and communication theory. In I. H. Angus & S. Jhally (eds.), *Cultural politics in contemporary America* (pp. 51–64). New York: Routledge.

Graber, D. A. (1989). *Mass media and American politics* (3rd edn.). Washington, DC: Congressional Quarterly Press.

Graber, D. A. (1988). *Processing the News* (2nd edn.). New York: Longman.

Gunter, B. (1987). *Poor reception: Misunderstanding and forgetting broadcast news*. Hillsdale, NJ: Lawrence Erlbaum.

Gusfield, J. (1989). The bridge over separated lands: Kenneth Burke's significance for the study of social action. In H. W. Simons & T. Melia (eds.), *The legacy of Kenneth Burke* (pp. 28–54). Madison: University of Wisconsin Press.

Gusfield, J. (1981). *The culture of public problems: Drinking-driving and the symbolic order*. Chicago: University of Chicago Press.

Haig, A. (1981, May). Interview for Spanish television. *Department of State Bulletin*, pp. 7–9.

Hall, S. (1984). The narrative construction of reality. *Southern Review*, *17*, 3–17.

Hall, S. (1982). The rediscovery of "ideology": The return of the repressed in media studies. In M. Gurevitch, T. Bennett, J. Curran, & S. Woollacott (eds.), *Culture, society, and the media* (pp. 56–90). London: Methuen.

Hall, S. (1980). Encoding/decoding. In S. Hall, D. Hobson, A. Lowe, & P. Willis (eds.), *Culture, media, language* (pp. 128–138). London: Hutchinson.

Hall, S. (1972). The determinations of news photographs. *Working Papers in Cultural Studies*, (3), Autumn. Birmingham: Centre for Critical Cultural Studies.

Hall, S., Critcher, C., Jefferson, T., Clarke, J., & Roberts, B. (1978). *Policing the crisis: Mugging, the state, and law and order*. New York: Holmes & Meier.

Hallin, D. C. (1985). The American news media: A critical theory perspective. In J. Forester (ed.), *Critical theory and public life* (pp. 121–146). Cambridge, MA: MIT Press.

Hallin, D. C., Manoff, R. K., & Weddle, J. K. (1989, November). *Sourcing patterns of key national security reporters: A case study in a structural determinant of discourse*. Paper presented at the Speech Communication Association Conference, San Francisco.

Hartley, J. (1982). *Understanding news*. London: Methuen.

Hauser, G. A. (1989). Administrative rhetoric and public opinion: Discussing the Iranian hostages in the public sphere. In T. W. Benson (ed.), *American rhetoric: context and criticism* (pp. 323–384). Carbondale, IL: Southern Illinois University Press.

Haynes, W. L. (1989). Shifting media, shifting paradigms, and the growing utility of narrative as metaphor. *Communication Studies*, *40*, 109–126.

Herman, E. S. (1982). *The real terror network*. Boston: South End Press.

Herman, E. S., & Chomsky, N. (1988). *Manufacturing consent: The political economy of the mass media*. New York: Pantheon.

Herman, E. S., & O'Sullivan, G. (1989). *The terrorism industry: The experts and institutions that shape our view of terror*. New York: Pantheon.

Hersh, S. M. (1987, Feb. 22). Target Qaddafi. *The New York Times Magazine*, pp. 17–84.

Hill, C. (1986). The political dilemmas for Western governments. In L. Freedman, C. Hill, A. Roberts, R. J. Vincent, P. Wilkinson, & P. Windsor (eds.), *Terrorism and international order* (pp. 77–100). New York: Routledge.

Hill, F. B. (1981, May). Media diplomacy: Crisis management with an eye on the TV screen. *Washington Journalism Review*, 23–27.

Hitchens, C. (1986, September). Wanton acts of usage. *Harper's*, pp. 66–70.

Howitt, D. (1982). *Mass media and social problems*. New York: Pergamon Press.

Hoynes, W., & Croteau, D. (1989). Are you on the Nightline guest list? *Extra!* 2(4), 2–25.

Iyengar, S., & Kinder, D. R. (1987). *News that matters*. Chicago: University of Chicago Press.

Jameson, F. (1984). Foreword to J. Lyotard, *The postmodern condition*. Minneapolis: University of Minnesota Press.

Jenkins, B. (1982). *Terrorism and beyond: An international conference on terrorism and low-level conflict*. Report prepared for the U.S. Department of Energy, the U.S. Department of Justice, and the U.S. Department of State. Santa Monica, CA: Rand Corporation (Publication no. R-2714-DOE/DOJ/DOS/RC).

Kampelman, M. M. (1981, April). Conference on Security and Cooperation in Europe addresses subject of terrorism. *Department of State Bulletin*, pp. 29–30.

Keen, S. (1986). *Faces of the enemy: Reflections of the hostile imagination*. New York: Harper & Row.

Kelly, M. J., & Mitchell, T. H. (1984). Transnational terrorism and the Western elite press. In D. A. Graber (ed.), *Media power in politics* (pp. 282–289). Washington, DC: Congressional Quarterly.

Kennedy, R. T. (1981, September). International terrorism. *Department of State Bulletin*, pp. 65–67.

Knight, G., & Dean, T. (1982). Myth and the structure of news. *Journal of Communication*, *32*(2), 44–61.

Kramer, M. (1987). The structure of Shi'ite terrorism. In A. Kurz (ed.), *Contemporary trends in world terrorism* (pp. 43–52). New York: Praeger.

Kupperman, R. H. (chair), (1986). *Combatting terrorism: A matter of leverage* (Panel report on terrorism, E. Marks & D. van Opstal (eds.)). Washington, DC: Georgetown University, Center for Strategic and International Studies.

Kupperman, R. H., & Kamen, J. (1989). *Final warning: Averting disaster in the new age of terrorism*. New York: Doubleday.

Laclau, E., & Mouffe, C. (1985). *Hegemony and socialist strategy*. Thetford, England: Thetford Press.

Laqueur, W. (1987). *The age of terrorism*. Boston: Little, Brown.

Lardner, G. (1991, May 6). Fewer bumps in the night. *The Washington Post National Weekly Edition*, p. 38.

Larson, J. F. (1986). Television and U.S. foreign policy: The other world war. *Journal of Communication*, *36*(4), 108–130.

Lasser, W. (1987). Fighting terrorism in democratic societies. In M. Slann & B. Schechterman (eds.), *Multidimensional terrorism* (pp. 111–120). Boulder, CO: Lynne Rienner.

Lee, M. A. (1989, March 15). State of terrorism address. *In These Times*, p. 18.

Leeman, R. W. (1988, November). *The rhetoric of terrorism*. Paper presented at the Speech Communication Association Conference, New Orleans.

Leeman, R. W. (1987). Rhetoric and values in terrorism. In M. Slann & B. Schechterman (eds.), *Multidimensional terrorism* (pp. 45–56). Boulder: Lynne Rienner.

Lewis, J. (1985). Decoding television news. In P. Drummond & R. Patterson (eds.), *Television in transition* (pp. 205–234). London: British Film Institute.

Livingstone, W. D. (1986). Terrorism and the media revolution. In T. E. Arnold (ed.), *Fighting back: Winning the war against terrorism* (pp. 213–227). Lexington, MA: D. C. Heath.

Lucaites, J. L., & Condit, C. M. (1990). Reconstructing <equality>: Culturetypal and counter-cultural rhetorics in the martyred black vision. *Communication Monographs, 57*, 5–24.

Lucaites, J. L., & Condit, C. M. (1985). Re-constructing narrative theory: A functional perspective. *Journal of Communication, 35*(4), 90–108.

Lule, J. (1988). The myth of my widow: A dramatistic analysis of news portrayals of a terrorist victim. *Political Communication and Persuasion, 5*, 101–120.

Lyotard, J. (1984). *The postmodern condition.* Minneapolis: University of Minnesota.

Marra, R. F., Ostrom, C. W., & Simon, D. M. (1990). Foreign policy and presidential popularity. *Journal of Conflict Resolution,* December, 588–623.

Mayer, J., & McManus, D. (1988). *Landslide: The unmaking of the president, 1984–1988.* Boston: Houghton Mifflin.

Martin, D. C., & Walcott, J. (1988). *Best laid plans: The inside story of America's war against terrorism.* New York: Simon & Schuster.

McGee, M. C. (1980). The "ideograph": A link between rhetoric and ideology. *Quarterly Journal of Speech, 66*, 1–16.

McGee, M. C., & Martin, M. A. (1983). Public knowledge and ideological argumentation. *Communication Monographs, 50*, 47–65.

Medhurst, M. J. (1989). Propaganda techniques in documentary film and television: AIM vs. PBS. In G. Burns & R. J. Thompson (eds.), *Television studies: Textual analysis* (pp. 183–204). New York: Praeger.

Merari, A., & Friedland, N. (1985). Social psychological aspects of political terrorism. In S. Oskamp (ed.), *International conflict and national public policy issues* (pp. 185–205). Beverly Hills, CA: Sage.

Mickolus, E. F., Sandler, T., & Murdock, J. M. (1989). *International terrorism in the 1980s,* vols. 1 and 2. Ames: Iowa University Press.

Miller, A. H. (ed.), (1982). *Terrorism, the media, and the law.* Dobbs Ferry, NY: Transnational.

Morgan, R. (1989). *The demon lover: On the sexuality of terrorism.* New York: W. W. Norton.

Morley, D. (1981). The nationwide audience: A critical postscript. *Screen Education, 39,* Summer, 3–14.

Morrison, P. R. (1986). Limits to technocratic consciousness: Information technology and terrorism as example. *Science, Technology, and Human Values, 11*(4), 4–16.

Morse, M. (1985). Talk, talk, talk—the space of discourse in television. *Screen, 26*(2), 2–17.

Mumby, D. K. (1989). Ideology and the social construction of meaning: A communication perspective. *Communication Quarterly, 37*, 291–304.

Murdock, G. (1982). Political deviance: The press presentation of a militant mass demonstration. In S. Cohen & J. Young (eds.), *The manufacture of news: Deviance, social problems, and the mass media* (pp. 206–225). Beverly Hills, CA: Sage.

Netanyahu, B. (1986). *Terrorism: How the West can win.* New York: Farrar, Strauss, Giroux.

Nichols, B. (1981). *Ideology and the image: Social representation in the cinema and other media.* Bloomington: Indiana University Press.

Nimmo, D., & Combs, J. E. (1985). *Nightly horrors: Crisis coverage by television network news.* Knoxville: University of Tennessee Press.

Nimmo, D., & Combs, J. E. (1983). *Mediated political realities.* New York: Longman.

Oakley, R. B. (1985a, June). Combatting international terrorism. *Department of State Bulletin*, pp. 73–78.

Oakley, R. B. (1985b, November). Terrorism: Overview and developments. *Department of State Bulletin*, pp. 61–65.

O'Ballance, E. (1979). *Language of violence: The blood politics of terrorism*. San Rafael, CA: Presidio Press.

O'Neill, M. J. (1986). *Terrorist spectaculars: Should TV coverage be curbed?* New York: Priority Press Publications.

O'Sullivan, J. (1986). Deny them publicity. In B. Netanyahu (ed.), *Terrorism: How the West can win* (pp. 120–125). New York: Farrar, Strauss, Giroux.

Palmerton, P. R. (1988). The rhetoric of terrorism and media response to the "Crisis in Iran." *Western Journal of Speech Communication, 52*, 105–121.

Paletz, D. L., Ayanian, J. Z., & Fozzard, P. A. (1982). Terrorism on TV news: The IRA, the FALN, and the Red Brigades. In W. C. Adams (ed.), *Television coverage of international affairs* (pp. 143–165). Norwood, NJ: Ablex.

Parenti, M. (1986). *Inventing reality: The politics of the mass media*. New York: St. Martin's Press.

Patterns of international terrorism: 1981 (1982, August). *Department of State Bulletin*, pp. 9–21.

Perdue, W. D. (1989). *Terrorism and the state*. New York: Praeger.

Perez, F. H. (1984). As quoted in S. Midgley & V. Rice (eds.), *Terrorism and the media in the 1980s*. Washington, DC: Media Institute.

Perez, F. H. (1982, January). The impact of international terrorism. *Department of State Bulletin*, pp. 55–57.

Picard, R. G. (1990). News coverage as the contagion of terrorism: Dangerous charges backed by dubious science. In D. A. Graber (ed.), *Media power in politics* (3rd edn.) (pp. 313–323). Washington, DC: Congressional Quarterly.

Press, C., & Verburg, K. (1988). *American politicians and journalists*. Glenview, IL: Scott, Foresman.

Provizer, N. W. (1987). Defining terrorism. In M. Slann & B. Schechterman (eds.), *Multi-dimensional terrorism* (pp. 3–10). Boulder, CO: Lynne Rienner.

Rachlin, A. (1988). *News as hegemonic reality: American political culture and the framing of news accounts*. New York: Praeger.

Reagan, R. (1985a). The president's news conferences of June 18, 1985. *Weekly Compilation of Presidential Documents, 21*, 806–811.

Reagan, R. (1985b, August). The new network of terrorist states. *Department of State Bulletin*, pp. 7–10.

Reagan, R. (1984a). Remarks following bombing near U.S. embassy annex in Beirut. *Weekly Compilation of Presidential Documents, 20*, 1317–1318.

Reagan, R. (1984b). International terrorism legislation, message to Congress, April 26, 1984. *Weekly Compilation of Presidential Documents, 20*, 590–593.

Reagan, R. (1984c). Statement by the president following the murder of Ray Hunt, February 21, 1984. *Weekly Compilation of Presidential Documents, 20*, 247.

Reagan, R. (1983a). Remarks following Pentagon report on the security of U.S. Marines in Lebanon, December 27, 1983. *Weekly Compilation of Presidential Documents, 19*, 1745–1747.

Reagan, R. (1983b, June). President's remarks, April 23, 1983. *Department of State Bulletin*, p. 61.

Ricoeur, P. (1976). *Interpretation theory: Discourse and the surplus of meaning*. Fort Worth, TX: Texas Christian University Press.

Roberts, A. (1986). Terrorism and international order. In L. Freedman, C. Hill, A. Roberts, R. J. Vincent, P. Wilkinson, & P. Windsor (eds.), *Terrorism and international order* (pp. 7–25). New York: Routledge.

Robinson, G. J. (1984). Television news and the claim to facticity. In W. D. Rowland & B. Watkins (eds.), *Interpreting television* (pp. 199–221). Beverly Hills, CA: Sage.

Rubin, J., & Friedland, N. (1986, July). Terrorists and their audience—theater of terror. *Current*, pp. 36–39.

Rubenstein, R. E. (1987). *Alchemists of revolution*. New York: Basic Books.

Said, E. W. (1988). The essential terrorist. In E. Said & C. Hitchens (eds.), *Blaming the victims* (pp. 149–158). New York: Verso.

Said, E. W. (1981). *Covering Islam*. New York: Pantheon Books.

Sayre, R. M. (1984, October). International terrorism: A long twilight struggle. *Department of State Bulletin*, pp. 48–49.

Schlesinger, P. (1981). "Terrorism," the media, and the liberal-democratic state: A critique of the orthodoxy. *Social Research*, Spring, 74–99.

Schlesinger, P., Murdock, G., & Elliott, P. (1983). *Televising terrorism: Political violence in popular culture*. London: Comedia Publishing Group.

Schmid, A. P., & de Graaf, J. (1982). *Violence as communication*. Beverly Hills, CA: Sage.

Schudson, M. (1986). When? Deadlines, datelines, and history. In R. K. Manoff & M. Schudson (eds.), *Reading the news* (pp. 79–108). New York: Pantheon.

Schudson, M. (1982). The politics of narrative form: The emergence of news conventions in print and television. *Daedalus*, *3*, 97–112.

Shaheen, J. G. (1984). *The TV Arab*. Bowling Green, KY: Bowling Green State University Popular Press.

Shaw, D. H., & McCombs, M. E. (1971). *The emergence of American political issues: The agenda-setting function of the press*. St. Paul, MN: West Publishing.

Shultz, G. (1986a). The challenge to democracy. In B. Netanyahu (ed.), *Terrorism: How the West can win* (pp. 16–24). New York: Farrar, Strauss, Giroux.

Shultz, G. (1986b, April). Foreign policy challenges. *Department of State Bulletin*, pp. 40–41.

Shultz, G. (1985a, December). Arms control, strategic stability, and global security. *Department of State Bulletin*, pp. 20–25.

Shultz, G. (1985b, August). Secretary's interview, "This Week With David Brinkley," June 23, 1985. *Department of State Bulletin*, pp. 77–81.

Shultz, G. (1984a, August). Terrorism: The problem and the challenge. *Department of State Bulletin*, pp. 29–34.

Shultz, G. (1984b, December). Terrorism and the modern world. *Department of State Bulletin*, pp. 12–17.

Shultz, G. (1984c, May). Power and diplomacy in the 1980s. *Department of State Bulletin*, pp. 12–15.

Shultz, G. (1983, December). The situation in Lebanon. *Department of State Bulletin*, pp. 44–45.

Simon, J. D. (1987). Misunderstanding terrorism. *Foreign Policy, 67*, Summer, 104–120.

Slater, R. O., & Stohl, M. (eds.), (1988). *Current perspectives on international terrorism*. New York: St. Martin's Press.

Smith, B. H. (1981). Narrative versions, narrative theories. In W.J.T. Mitchell (ed.), *On narrative* (pp. 209–232). Chicago: University of Chicago Press.

Smith, L. D. (1989). A narrative analysis of the party platforms: The Democrats and Republicans of 1984. *Communication Quarterly, 37*, 91–99.

Smith, L. D. (1988). Narrative styles in network coverage of the 1984 nominating conventions. *Western Journal of Speech Communication, 52*, 63–74.

Sofaer, A. D. (1985, October). Fighting terrorism through law. *Department of State Bulletin*, pp. 38–39.

Sperry, S. (1981). Television news as narrative. In R. P. Adler (ed.), *Understanding television* (pp. 292–312). New York: Praeger.

Sterling, C. (1981). *The terror network: The secret war of international terrorism*. New York: Holt, Rinehart, and Winston.

Stevenson, C. L. (1963). *Facts and values: Studies in ethical analysis*. New Haven, CT: Yale University Press.

Stohl, M. (1988). Responding to the terrorist threat: Fashions and fundamentals. In R. O. Slater & M. Stohl (eds.), *Current perspectives on international terrorism*. New York: St. Martin's Press.

Tan, Z.C.W. (1989, May). *Antithesis of responsible journalism—insurgent terrorism in the pre-media and post-media eras*. Paper presented at the International Communication Association, San Francisco.

Tan, Z.C.W. (1988). Media publicity and insurgent terrorism: A twenty-year balance sheet. *Gazette, 42*, 3–32.

Tan, Z.C.W. (undated). *The role of media in insurgent terrorism—issues and perspectives*. Unpublished manuscript. Department of Radio-TV-Film, University of Texas, Austin.

Targ, H. R. (1988). Societal structure and revolutionary terrorism: A preliminary investigation. In R. O. Slater & M. Stohl (eds.), *Current perspectives on international terrorism*. New York: St. Martin's Press.

Taylor, C. D. (1985, August). Links between international narcotics trafficking and terrorism. *Department of State Bulletin*, pp. 69–70.

Toloyan, K. (1989). Narrative culture and the motivation of the terrorist. In J. Shotter & K. J. Gergen (eds.), *Texts of identity* (pp. 99–118). London: Sage.

Toolan, M. J. (1988). *Narrative: A critical investigation*. New York: Routledge.

Tuchman, G. (1978). *Making news*. New York: Free Press.

Turner, G. (1988). *Film as social practice*. London: Routledge.

Vanderbilt Television News Archive. The Jean and Alexander Heard Library, Vanderbilt University, Nashville, TN.

van Dijk, T. A. (1988). *News analysis: Case studies of international and national news in the press*. Hillsdale, NJ: Lawrence Erlbaum.

van Dijk, T. A. (1988). *News as discourse*. Hillsdale, NJ: Lawrence Erlbaum.

Viera, J. D. (1988). Terrorism at the BBC: The IRA on British television. *Journal of Film and Video, 40*, 28–36.

Vought, D. B., & Fraser, J. H. (1986, July). Terrorism: The search for working definitions. *Military Review*, 71–76.

Wagner-Pacifici, R. E. (1986). *The Moro morality play: Terrorism as social drama.* Chicago: University of Chicago Press.

Wallis, R., & Baran, S. J. (1990). *The known world of broadcast news.* New York: Routledge.

Wardlaw, G. (1988). State responses to international terrorism: Some cautionary comments. In R.O. Slater & M. Stohl (eds.), *Current perspectives on international terrorism* (pp. 206–245). New York: St. Martin's Press.

Warnick, B. (1987). The narrative paradigm: Another story. *Quarterly Journal of Speech, 73*, 197–204.

Weaver, P. (1981). TV news and newspaper news. In R. P. Adler (ed.), *Understanding television* (pp. 277–294). New York: Praeger.

Weimann, G. (1987). Media events: The case of international terrorism. *Journal of Broadcasting and Electronic Media, 31*, 21–39.

Weimann, G. (1985). Terrorists or freedom fighters? Labeling terrorism in the Israeli press. *Political Communication and Persuasion, 2*, 433–445.

Weimann, G. (1983). The theater of terror: Effects of press coverage. *Journal of Communication, 33*(1), 38–45.

White, H. (1981). The narrativization of real events. In W.J.T. Mitchell (ed.), *On narrative* (pp. 249–254). Chicago: University of Chicago Press.

Whitehead, J. C. (1987, February). Terrorism: The challenge and the response. *Department of State Bulletin*, pp. 70–73.

Wilkinson, P. (1986). Trends in international terrorism and the American response. In L. Freedman, C. Hill, A. Roberts, R. J. Vincent, P. Wilkinson, & P. Windsor (eds.), *Terrorism and international order* (pp. 37–55). New York: Routledge.

Wittebols, J. (1990). "Terror" across the border: U.S. and Canadian use of a buzzword. *Extra, 3*(5), 11.

Woodward, B. (1987). *Veil: The secret wars of the CIA, 1981–1987.* New York: Simon & Schuster.

Yang, F. (1990, October). The political landscape. *Campaign*, p. 15.

Yardley, J. (1990, March 5). Not all the news we can use. (Review of F. Graham's *Happy Talk: Confessions of a TV Newsman*). *Washington Post National Weekly Edition*, p. 36.

Index

ABOUT THE AUTHOR

BETHAMI A. DOBKIN is Director of Media Studies and Assistant Professor of Communication Studies at the University of San Diego. She has published and spoken on the news media and foreign policy since 1988.